Jean-Pierre Panouillé

The City of Carcassonne

Illustrated by Gérard Guillier

Photos by André Panouillé
        Hervé Champollion

Translated by Angela Moyon

ouest france

caisse nationale
des monuments
historiques
et des sites

Ministère de la Culture

The region

The towers of the walled town are like observation posts looking out over a variety of landscapes.

To the North, the ponderous outline of the Montagne Noire and its dark forests are a foretaste of the Massif Central. To the South, the horizon is blocked by the Corbières and the first peaks in the Pyrénées. Bordered by these two mountain ranges, the narrow corridor controlled by Carcassonne is a link between the Mediterranean and Atlantic coasts. To the West, wide pastures, corn, barley, maize, and more recently sunflowers all lead to the Lauragais, the « Gateway to Aquitaine ». To the East lies the Mediterranean, the South of France, with its vineyards and arid oak woods.

Be careful when you walk round the walls. You will almost certainly have to battle against the wind; it is a constant feature of Carcassonne's weather. The « Marin », or South Wind blows in from the Mediterranean. It is a greasy, damp, sticky grey wind that brings with it an overcast sky and mild, dull weather. Or it may be a black gale that sends heavy clouds loaded with rain scudding overhead. From the North comes the fresh, clear, invigorating Cers that sometimes has quite a bite to it. As to the West winds, they bring persistent drizzle from the Atlantic.

A meander of the R. Aude flows down below. At this point, it no longer flows in the South-North direction it has followed since it rose in the Pyrenees; instead, it bends Eastwards until it reaches the Mediterranean.

The present town of Carcassonne

Front cover:
The defences of the Count's castle *: built during the first half of the 13th Century, the walls and towers which "encase" the former dispossessed Viscounts' Palace were probably erected to ensure the safety of the royal troops who were stationed there from 1226 onwards and who « occupied » the surrounding country. This is one of the main turning points in the history of Carcassonne. The feudal town was to become a major royal fortress.
* The Barracks and Major Towers.

Back cover:
The side aisles and nave in St.Nazaire's Church: the ribbed cradle vault in the nave and the semicircular arches in the narrow side aisles which are almost as high provide mutual support and bring perfect harmony to the building. This system prevented any direct entry of light into the nave thereby making the interior very dark in the Romanesque cathedral that was begun in 1096 and completed in the mid 12th Century.

The West end of the town: the view towards the Montagne Noire. In the foreground stands the so-called Inquisition Tower, or round Bishop's Tower, on which the restoration work is plainly visible on the upper storey just below the roof. The Bishop's Palace used to be next to this tower and the Bishop was also granted permission to use several rooms in the towers flanking his palace. In the middle distance is the castle.

Overleaf:
A general view of the South side: The town as the classicists saw it, encircled by ramparts, towering over the countryside.

stretches along an alluvial terrace formed over the years by the river. The walled town occupies the tip of a small plateau with fairly steeply-sloping sides above the R. Aude (a drop of some 490 ft.) and more gentle slopes on the East side.

The sandstone crops out in many places at the foot of the walls. This is the rock that was used to build the walls and the towers. Its scientific name is Carcassonne molasse. It was quarried either on the plateau itself or in the surrounding hills.

An oppidum on the main overland route from the Atlantic to the Mediterranean

The oldest known traces of human life on the mound date from the 6th Century B.C.

Cob or wattle huts, larder-silos buried in the ground, a few craftsmen's workshops e.g. a potter's kiln, and pens in which to keep animals were all that existed on the mound overlooking the R. Aude in those days. These rudimentary constructions of which archaeologists have uncovered a few remains constituted an oppidum, i.e.. a hillfort, perhaps protected by a dry stone wall. At this time, similar communities were springing up on rises throughout the South of Gaul. For the inhabitants of these forts, it was not only a question of improving security but also of keeping watch over passing foreign traders and gaining financial advantage from this commercial traffic. Phocaeans from Marseilles, Adge or Ampurias were travelling inland in ever-increasing numbers and Carcassonne, which stood at the junction of two major roads, was in a particularly privileged position.

To the South, the upper Aude Valley and the Pyrenean passes lead to Catalonia; to the North, the Massif Central lay at the end of the trails through the Montagne Noire. More importantly, however, the walled town towered over the great East-West road across the Naurouze Ridge and through the Carcassonne Corridor, the shortest overland route between the Atlantic and the Mediterranean.

This was one of the tin routes. The metal was vital for the manufacture of bronze and people travelled as far as Cornwall to get it. Greek, Etruscan or Carthaginian wares were taken to Tou-

Gallo-Roman towers on the North wall (the Samson and Avar Mill Towers): there are no windows on the ground floor, and these towers have two levels of defence. Wide windows enabled troops to throw javelins and use their slings. The gently-sloping roofs are now covered with fluted tiles (or South of France tiles) which resemble the Roman « tegulae ». The rubble and brick-chained facing is typical of the Lower Empire's building.

The North Gate in the foreground, which used to lead to the suburb of Saint-Vincent, was not provided with any particular system of defence after the suburb itself disappeared, but it was certainly walled up if danger threatened.

louse and the communities along the Atlantic coast. Some of these products were offered to the earliest inhabitants of Carcassonne, as is shown by the remains of amphorae and the fragments of pottery found buried in the walled town. This business activity was to ensure a certain level of prosperity for the hillfort of which present excavations carried out in difficult conditions on the outskirts of the town do not really give a true picture.

The Tectosages: « Modest and unpretentious » despite their wealth

The Tectosages, who came from Central Europe c. 300 B.C., conquered the Iberians of Languedoc. Although they were relatively few in number, they constituted a military aristocracy who took control of hilltop villages and erected fortifications, or improved those already in existence. According to the Greek geographer Strabo who was writing in the early years A.D., the Tectosages lived « modestly and unpretentiously ». They feared the gods and accumulated enormous quantities of gold and silver for them in the form of bars and jewellery.

Did the Tectosages in Carcassonne have a fabulous treasure trove, like their counterparts in Toulouse? It is more than likely. « The land they occupy is brimming over with gold », said Strabo and although he may well have been exaggerating slightly, he was not telling a downright lie. Archaeologists have shown that in the 2nd Century B.C. the precious metal was extracted from the Montagne Noire as it still is today, in Salsigne. Miners' lamps have been found in some of the tunnels dug out at this time at a distance of no more than twelve miles from Carcassonne.

Despite their gold, the Tectosages « banished all luxury from their life ». They grew cereal crops and ground the grain on millstones that originally worked on a forward-and-back principle before the invention of rotating millstones. They bred goats, sheep, and pigs, and hunted stags, wild boar, and the small game that filled the thickets in the Corbières.

They also proved to be excellent craftsmen. The everyday handmade pottery with its crude cut decorations gave way to thrown pots made of finer clay with more delicate designs.

A small Gallo-Roman town on the wine route

In the year 122 B.C., the Consul Domitius Ahenobarbus travelled through the territory he had conquered, viz. Provence and Languedoc. The elephant on which he liked to appear and the discipline of his troops impressed the people. The distant authority of Rome was accepted without any great difficulty.

A Roman road soon passed below the hillfort at Carcassonne, linking Narbonne and Toulouse. It quickly became a major wine route, for the Gauls were very fond of the drink and the owners of the great estates in Southern Italy exported their production by the shipload to the port of Narbonne. In one of Cicero's texts, there is a list of the toll offices along the road in the days of the governor Fonteius. Despite the deformation of the name, it seems that one of the towns listed was indeed Carcasso. Merchants had to pay a tax equivalent to approximately 50 % of the value of every amphorae of wine transported. The people of Carcassonne also drank Italian wine, as is proved by the fragments of Campanian amphorae discovered in the walled town, but they began to show an increasing preference for the wines from their own vineyards. Wine-growing was to spread throughout the Languedoc Region in the last few years B.C.

Carcassonne was too near Narbonne, the provincial capital, to become a major administrative and economic centre. Instead, it remained a medium-sized town after the Conquest of Gaul by Julius Ceasar.

The town must have been elevated to the rank of colony at the beginning of the Christian era *(Colonia Julia Carcasso)* and Pliny the Elder classified it among the « latina oppida ». There is no doubt whatsoever that it was a fortified town, although the exact type of fortification erected is not clear. During the Roman occupation, the houses became increasingly comfortable. The floors were tiled, the walls were given a coating of stucco, and the thatch and branch roofs were replaced by flat tiles with rims (tegulae) and curved tiled joints (imbrices). In the courtyard of the Count's castle, there are rooms from a house with mosaic floors. The decoration is simple but nevertheless displays a certain amount of luxury.

The name of only one Carcassonnais has come down through History. He was a modest legionary called Caïus Julius Niger, who died at the age of 45 after 17 years service on the Rhine, in Mainz, to which he went in the middle of the 1st Century A.D. with the IInd Legion.

Facing up to brigands and barbarians : the Lower Empire wall

In the 3rd Century A.D., the defences of the Empire's frontiers on which the good Caïus Julius had served so peaceably one hundred and fifty years previously crumbled beneath the attacks of the Germanic tribes.

After the devastation of the Barbarians who were more interested in pillaging at that time than in conquering territory, came the dangers of the Bagauds or groups of deserters, small landowners and urban workers who had been ruined by all the destruction (or by the inflation that successive Emperors had been unable to control).

As a safety measure, the inhabitants of a large number of the towns in Gaul began building walls. In 333 A.D., the itinerary of a pilgrim travelling from Bordeaux to Jerusalem describes Car-

cassonne as a « castellum », i.e. fortress town. Some sections of the present inner wall are typical of the military architecture of the Lower Empire, and are no doubt the remains of these early fortifications.

The foundations of a Gallo-Roman wall are not very deep (approximately 3-6 ft). They consist of two or three layers of blocks of stones, perhaps from a previous wall, often completed by a thick layer of very hard mortar. The walls are 6 ft.6 ins. - 10 ft. thick. The facing (small stones) is broken up by brick chaining designed to level up the wall and improve cohesion. Between the two faced sides, most of the thickness comes from a layer of mortar containing pebbles, gravel or broken tiles. The mortar used was a mixture of one-third limestone and two-thirds sand to which crushed brick was often added. Its legendary solidity doubtless comes from the correct firing of the limestone and careful ramming down to avoid any air bubbles. A crenelated parapet walk ran round the walls some 26 ft. above ground level but the alterations carried out in the Middle Ages always did away with these upper sections. In order to be able to « attack the side of the enemy forces undertaking the assault of the walls », as the Roman Vegetius advised, the towers were flat on the town side from which there was no danger but built with a semicircular forework facing the open country. The shape offered excellent resistance to battering rams and made possible a variety of angles of fire. The lower section was complete and was designed to reinforce the wall. On the first floor three semicircular windows with brick archstones opened onto the country; they were large enough to leave room for the throwing of the « pilum », the Romans' favourite weapon (a sort of big javelin) or the use of a sling. The upper, floored storey was defended by battlements which were designed to support a gently-sloping roof (tiles could not be fixed on a roof with too steep a slope). The Romans were not very familiar with the bow so there were no slit-windows. As the missiles used had only a limited range, the towers were no more than 98 ft. apart. All defence was therefore based on two principles, firstly the repelling of attack by the thickness and solidity of the walls and secondly the inflicting of heavy losses on the enemy by showering missiles down on them vertically from the top of the walls and from the towers.

The double line of defences along the South wall : two constructions designed by the royal architects of the 13th Century. Firstly, there is the flat, regular outer wall of medium-sized rubble which was doubtless built between 1230 and 1240. Then there is the inner wall with its bossed rubble, built c. 1280 to replace the old Gallo-Roman wall.

Overleaf:
The Narbonnaise Gate : built between 1280 and 1287, it defended the main Eastern entrance to the town, facing the Narbonne direction. The fake drawbridge in the foreground is a fanciful piece of restoration work. Originally, the gate doubtless had a plain wooden footbridge which could easily be removed in case of danger. The moats were never filled with water but their depth constituted an obstacle for attackers that was difficult to overcome. Slightly further North, the Tréseau Tower complete the mighty defences that were made necessary by the lie of the land. Its gentle slope provided very poor protection.

The Gallo-Roman wall was simply reinforced on the North side. To the South, it was replaced by more modern fortifications which rejoined it in several places to the East and West. Its layout more or less followed that of the present inner wall. The only place where the two walls follow a separate line is between the Constable's Mill Tower and the Narbonnaise Gate where the Gallo-Roman construction is quite visible, set back from the mediaeval wall.

Within a half-mile perimeter, the Lower Empire wall enclosed a town with an area of just over seventeen acres. Its size and appearance were reminiscent of the walls in Le Mans or Senlis which were also built at this time, i.e. in the late 3rd or early 4th Centuries. Were the walls and towers any help in fighting off the great invasions of the late 4th and early 5th Centuries? At least they often had the advantage of preventing pillage and wholesale massacre and allowing the inhabitants to negotiate an honourable surrender.

The Franks v. the Visigoths, the Saracens v. Charlemagne: the birth of legends

The Visigoths, natives of the Danube river valley, first crossed Italy then, in the 5th Century, conquered Spain and Languedoc. According to Gregory of Tours, it was in Carcassonne that they hid their treasure, away from the greedy eyes of the Franks. The treasure came from the sack of Rome by Alaric. « The admirable candlesticks of Solomon, King of the Hebrews, vases decorated with precious stones that the Romans had once taken from Jerusalem » and many other treasures were said to have been hidden in the town well. Some citizens of Carcassonne still believed this in the early 19th Century; they founded an association with the declared aim of emptying out the great well and finding the famous trove. With or without these riches, Carcassonne seems to have been one of the Franks' main targets in their attempts to push the Visigoths back across the Pyrenees. In 508 A.D., Clovis failed. In 584 A.D., King Gontran, who could not accept that « the frontiers of these dreadful Goths should lie within the territory of the Gauls », sent his best soldiers to attack Carcassonne. But the « town's excellent position enabled it to resist for a long time ».

The Vade Tower: built in 1245 on the site of the suburb of Saint-Michel which had been razed to the ground after the revolt in 1240, this tower is totally independent of the outer wall. It has its own well, bread oven, fireplaces and latrines. The spiral staircase leading to the upper storeys was cut directly into the wall. In some ways, the Vade Tower is reminiscent of the Constance Tower in Aigues-Mortes which was also built during this period.

At the beginning of the 8th Century, Carcassonne had to ward off attack by the Saracens. In the spring of 725 A.D., the Moslem governor of Spain, Anbasa Ibn Suhaym al Kalbi (whom chroniclers call simply Ambisa) overran the town, took a large amount of booty and carried off some of the inhabitants as slaves. The town was given an Arab garrison and renamed Karkashuna. However in 759, the Arabs were hounded out of Septimanca by Pippin the Short and pushed back across the Pyrenees.

This brief Saracen occupation inspired mediaeval writers to create picturesque legends of which Charlemagne is, of course, the hero. The Emperor besieged the town held by Dame Carcas, a Moslem princess. Time passed, and all that was left to feed the population was a small pig and one measure of corn.

Convinced of the effectiveness of psychological warfare, Dame Carcas fattened up the piglet with the last measure of corn and sent the replete podgy animal over the wall. The Emperor decided not to continue the siege of a town where food was still so plentiful that it was used to nettle the enemy. As Charlemagne was setting off at the head of his army, Dame Carcas had the trumpet sounded (a play on the French « Carcassonne » or « Carcas is ringing ») and proposed a peace treaty to the Emperor who had turned back to meet her.

When the great Emperor's legendary gesture is not being used for etymological purposes, it helps to explain certain architectural curiosities. « God showed his authority by bending one of the towers over as Charlemagne approached. It can still be seen today. This is how he was able to take the town ».

Although legends about these far-distant days are particularly numerous, very few documents have been handed down to us. They teach us little about the early days of the feudal system in Carcassonne and only the names of the first counts (Oliba, Acfred, Roger, Raymond etc.) conjure up a picture of these times.

*The strategic importance of Carcassonne at the Northernmost tip of the Visigoths' kingdom led early historians to believe that the remains of the rubble and brick chain wall were built by them. They were, however, not good builders. They are said to have copied the Lower Empire's building techniques or to have employed a local work force. The hypothesis of this Visigoths' wall was totally rejected, but has recently been revived, somewhat hesitatingly, by mediaeval experts. It would be just as logical to suppose that the sections of the Gallo-Roman wall which were considered to be too weak or in bad condition were rebuilt by the Visigoths.

The West wall of the castle : The Pint Tower on the right was a watchtower. In the centre are the castle lodgings which blend into the inner town wall. In the foreground is a section of the wall of the great barbican, a forework which has partially disappeared today. A circular defensive wall at the foot of the mound is linked to the castle by a covered passage (i.e. a passage flanked by two battlemented walls) as shown in this photo.

Skilful powerful lords: the Trencavels

Everything began with a seizure of power. In 1082, Bernard Aton Trencavel, Viscount of Albi, Nîmes and Béziers, proclaimed himself Viscount of Carcassonne. Although he was related on his mother's side to the former dynasty which had died out without any direct descendents, Bernard Aton was nevertheless not the rightful heir. However, the house of Barcelona who had paid off death duties on the Carcasses and Razes Regions (a goodly sum was involved) was in the grip of family struggles and was in no state to react. After two serious disputes with his subjects, Bernard Aton was finally able to impose his authority. Forty small lords of the surrounding « castra » (fortified villages or castles) rebelled in 1120 and were promptly dispossessed of their lands. Their goods were used to reward loyal men who became the viscount's new vassals. From then on, the Trencavels were to be solidly ensconced in Carcassonne for nigh on one hundred years. Their power, which divisions of the estate on a number of occasions did little to diminish, was inferior only to that of the two great rival houses who were attempting to gain supremacy over the whole of the South of France, viz. Toulouse and Barcelona.

After marriage had united the County of Barcelona and the Kingdom of Aragon, King Alphonse II ruled the Pyrenees, and his descendents sought to widen their sphere of influence to the whole of Languedoc and beyond, to Provence.

The exploits of Raymond de Saint-Gilles, Count of Toulouse, during the First Crusade reinforced his family's prestige and the size of their estate made it quite plausible to think that the Counts of Toulouse might head a great Southern state.

The Trencavels took advantage of the complex feudal links binding them to these two powerful rival neighbours and were quick to ask for support from Toulouse when their authority was being called into question in Barcelona, or help from the King of Aragon if they were in dispute with the Counts of Toulouse. Skilfully remaining their own masters, the Trencavels ruled over some sixty knights in the viscountcies of Béziers and Carcassonne alone, if one is to believe a charter drawn up in 1191. This was only a fraction of the loyal subjects on whom they could rely, but it already represented a considerable force even when compared to the kingdom as a whole.

The walled town of Carcassonne was divided into sixteen castellanies. A loyal aristocrat would be responsible for a section of the wall, usually comprising one or two towers. The nobleman had to live in a house within the town, with his family and servants; this was known as the « service de l'estage » (or « floor service »). In exchange for services rendered in protecting the town, the lord of the manor received lands outwith the town and a number of privileges.

The tilt-yard and passage beneath the square Bishop's Tower: by throwing objects down through the machicolations (or trap doors), the defending forces could knock out the enemy cowering beneath the archway. Moreover, the narrowness of the tilt-yard made it easy to set up barricades and spread the defences over several areas.

The castle in the days of the troubadours

Like all the great feudal lords of their day, the Trencavels enjoyed adventure and long rides. Bernard Aton took part in the First Crusade, spending four years in Palestine. In 1118, « to honour a vow », he set off to fight the Moors in Spain. It is probably his feats of warfare that inspired the frescoes in one of the rooms in the castle, the only remaining trace of mediaeval decoration. It was in this room, which « the regular visitors to the castle called the Round Chamber, although it was rectangular », that the Trencavels dealt with everyday business. They received homage from their vassals « in the Great Chamber » or, more often « beneath the elm tree in the courtyard of the palace ».

Most of the buildings back onto the Gallo-Roman wall. To the North was a chapel which has since disappeared, and to the South a watchtower. A huge room was set square to this row of buildings, and the living quarters therefore had a right-angled layout. Some of the buildings we see today have been raised. The former roof of « lauzes » (thick schist slabs) and the layout of the battlements above it can been seen quite clearly halfway up the present walls. Wide bay windows have replaced most of the narrow slits which let very little light into the rooms. The interior of the « Palatium » underwent major alteration over the years and now gives few indications of what life was like in feudal days. The purpose for which the various rooms were used is also largely unknown. The walls were frequently painted, the floors were covered with flagstones or tiles, and there was little furniture (chests, tables, and benches). Yet luxury did exist. A charter dated 1150 mentions « The viscount's rich wardrobe, his gold and silver jewellery, his vases, beds, carpets, wall-hangings, tablecloths and other similar items... ».

Troubadours and minstrels were frequent guests in the castle. Ramon de Miraval advises his juggler to « take root in the Carcassès Region... I shall not name all the barons... for it is difficult to choose among such a courteous group ». Peire Vidal admits to « great joy in the company of the ladies of the Carcassès whose actions and behaviour are pleasing to him, as are those of the knights, barons and Vavasours of the region ».

The wife of Roger II (Viscount from 1167 to 1194), Azalaïs or Adelaïde de Burlats, received the homage of Pons de la Garde, Guiraud de Salignac and Arnault de Maruelh who told her of his dreams. « I close my eyes and sigh, and fall asleep sighing. Then, Madame, my spirit flies straight to you whom it longs to see. And just as I should like to do myself, night and day whenever I think of it, it pays you homage, embraces you, kisses you and caresses you... » However, the unfortunate poet was rejected, and replaced by a high-ranking admirer, none other than the King of Aragon.

Were these relationships purely Platonic in the days of the Courts of Love, those courtly schools in which subjects such as « Can love exist between married partners ? » were debated ? René Nelli, one of the finest specialists in the field of Occitan literature, is far from convinced.

The refined lifestyle, the cosmopolitan court of Jewish scholars and poets from Aquitaine, Provence and Spain, existed only because the Trencavels were rich. Their lands provided them with substantial income but they also acquired revenue from all kinds of taxes and tolls. They reserved sole rights, for example, on the sale of salt and the warehouse where the precious merchandise was stored was a source of profit, as were the ovens, mills, and presses which they owned. The deniers, decorated on one side with the crescent moon and on the back with a crozier, which were made in the workshop near the Mint Tower and which bore the family's name, typify the economic power of the great feudal lords.

Day-to-day life in Carcassonne

The town was prosperous. Two annual fairs, one in the spring and the other in autumn, attracted not only merchants from the South of France but also Italians and Spaniards. Among the goods sold were woollen sheets famed for their durability, all types of skins and hides, knives, sheep-shearing equipment, and a variety of metal instruments. People brought cereals, wine, almonds, herbs gathered in the Corbières and the Montagne Noire, local farm produce, and articles made by local craftsmen, to sell at the fairs. During the town's heyday, the inhabitants ate well of course. Food in 12th-century Carcassonne was quite plentiful and varied. The bread which formed the staple diet was usually made from wheat. It was made in the form of a large round loaf, a flat pancake-shaped loaf, or a bannock. People also made a sort of waffle called an « oublie ». The commonest meat was salt pork but the butchers in Carcassonne also provided beef for those who could afford it. Lawyers and other members of the judiciary often received geese or capons in payment for their services and chicken broth was a delicacy that was served to the sick. The many days of fasting imposed by the Church explains the importance of fish, whether freshwater or sea, in the diet of the day. Pike, raw salmon, salt mullet, hake, eel, and trout were all common. There was also fried food, e.g. fish, eggs, meatballs, or simply bread. The usual vegetables were cabbage, turnips and swedes, broad beans, lentils, split peas,

onions, and leeks. The food was cooked in earthenware pots (the « olla »), in cauldrons (the « payrola »), or in frying pans (the « patella »), and was heavily seasoned with pepper. To end the meal, there was ewe's milk cheese and fruit such as grapes, figs, apples, pears, quince, cherries, strawberries, and walnuts. People drank wine of course, often watered down, and a type of plonk called « brout ». Although the poorest families had to be content with chestnuts, the rich had dates, ginger, cane sugar, and figs in honey. In the early years of the 13th Century, a poor carpenter making looms earned 8 deniers a day. To celebrate the fair properly and forget his usual fare of salt pork braised with cabbage in an earthenware pot, he could buy himself two eels (6 deniers) or a large portion of fish pâté (5 deniers). And the rest he could spend at his will in one of the many taverns in the town.

From one week before the start of the fairs to one week after they had ended, security was ensured throughout the Viscount's territory by armed detachments of men paid by the Trencavels. The family was also wise enough (or perhaps it was a result of public pressure) to put an end to their high-handed use of authority. No exceptional tax could be levied without the consent of the local dignitaires. The people of Carcassonne could divide out their estate as they wished by means of a will, and the money raised on the sale of salt, fish, corn, and meat no longer depended on the Viscount; the taxes were

established according to a charter. Another written document published « beneath the elm tree in front of the palace », controlling business between creditors and debtors, was based on Roman law. It also described the workings of the lord's justice. Questions of administration, justice, and taxation were settled by a Provost, a sort of palace official who soon acquired an assistant or sub-Provost. However, twelve annually-elected arbiters controlled and administered the affairs of the town, defending its rights, privileges and liberties in the face of opposition from the Viscount's people.

How many inhabitants were these dignitaries, who were soon to given the title of Consul, supposed to represent? There are no texts to prove it but a rough estimate would put the total population living within the single town wall at no more than several hundred.

The town and its suburbs in the 12th Century: a rapidly-expanding urban community

In the days of the Trencavels, there were two large villages outside the walled town. The oldest was apparently Saint-Michel, originally known as Castellare. It lay at the Southern end of the plateau. The present cemetery in front of the Narbonnaise Gate is an extension of the graveyard that was once adjacent to St. Michael's Church which was built « close by the walls of Carcassonne ». The Razès Gate, which stood on almost the same spot as today's Saint-Nazaire Gate, connected this suburb to the town. On the hillside to the North lay Saint-Vincent. The houses huddled round the church of the same name (which has now disappeared) and round St. Mary's Church, now called the Church of Our Lady of the Abbey. The northern gate, which is still known as the village gate, led to this second suburb.

Near the great well in the walled town: a narrow alley leads to the square on which stands the great well and to the castle. Behind each house is a yard, a garden or an orchard. The inhabitants provided some of their own food by growing vegetables, raising poultry and pigs, and tending their fig- or almond-trees.

Overleaf:
The South front: a protected section of wall along which all building is forbidden provides a view of the walled town amidst the vineyards and orchards. During recent restoration projects, Bourguignon (or flat) tiled roofs similar to those thought to have been erected by royal architects in the 13th Century have gradually replaced the slate used by Viollet-le-Duc in the 19th Century.

Both villages were surrounded by « walls, towers and moats ». The place at which the Saint-Vincent wall joined the main wall of Carcassonne is still visible today beside the Avar Mill Tower. Gates like the Salt-works and Almond-tree Gates opened either into the country-side or into a less serried form of urban development with alternating houses, vineyards, vegetable patches and pastures (« ferratjals » in Occitan). This was « suburbium ». Between the walled town and the R. Aude, there were numerous new buildings which gradually formed a new village called Granoillant or Graveillant.

Just before the crusade against the Albigensians, c. 1200, the hillside below the town walls was covered with churches, bourgeois houses, more modest dwellings, garden huts, work-shops, and salt and wool warehouses. The mills along the course of the Aude provided the community's flour. Water was not in short supply. There was the river, the Fontgrande spring in Saint-Michel, and another spring which rose close to the Aude Gate. The sandstone forming the mound on which the town was built was very permeable, but there were a few deposits of clay at various levels forming natural pockets of water which were veritable reservoirs. It would be surprising indeed if, among the twenty or so wells that exist today in the town, at least one had not been dug way back in the mists of time.

To the 12th-century pilgrim or merchant from the North, Carcassonne was not so much a fortress as a wealthy town on the road to Spain and the Mediterranean. After crossing the Aude by the one wooden bridge, he would have to cross the suburbs which retained an air of rusticity, enter one of the two fortified villages, and climb up the bustling busy alleys to the old Gallo-Roman wall whose thickness and solidity were so impressive. Beyond it, above this urban community that bore witness to the economic vitality of the region, stood the walled town and the aristocratic houses that protected it, the Viscount's castle, the Bishop's palace, the canons' house and cloisters, and the newly-completed St-Nazaire's Cathedral.

It was on 11th June 1099 that Pope Urban II blessed the stones that had been prepared for the building of St.Nazaire's Cathedral. It was finished in the first third of the 12th Century. At the end of the 13th Century, a Gothic transept and chancel were to replace the Romanesque chevet of which only the crypt still remains. Today, all that is left of the Romanesque cathedral is the ribbed barrel vaulting in the nave supported by the semicircular arches in the narrow side aisles. Then, as now, people entered the cathedral by the North Door which is on a level with the third span. The tympanum may well have been painted, as was perhaps the arching that rests on colonettes. The sculptures have been restored fairly exactly; the battlements above the West Front giving the impression that the Romanesque cathedral was fortified, are in fact a rather unhappy 19th-century addition.

The inner and outer walls (South side): not only two rows of fortifications but also different levels. The inner wall, which is always the higher of the two, « controls » the outer wall. At no point should the outer wall block the view.
The towers in the outer wall are « open at the gorge », i.e. open on the town side. Should the enemy manage to capture this first line of defence, there is no shelter available and the troops therefore come under fire from the defenders on the inner wall.

The Cathars in Carcassonne

A few years after the cathedral was built, Catharism spread through the town « like a cancerous growth ».

The origins of the Cathar religion are doubtless to be found in the old Manichean doctrines of the East. The merchants, pilgrims and crusaders who travelled through Dalmatia and the Balkans discovered the religious dualism of the Bogomiles. Finding this simple clear vision of the world much to their liking (Good on one side, Evil on the other), they became the propagators of a revised form of Christianity which was corrected by their Bulgarian intermediaries and they were nicknamed « Bulgars ». The Cathars believed in two types of creation. There were « all things invisible and immaterial, which are the work of God », and « all things visible and material, which are the work of the Devil ». Such ideas lead of course to a refusal of the material world. Although the moral code was fairly lax for the majority of the believers, the « Perfects » or « pure ones » lived totally detached from all temporal satisfactions. So as not to do evil, they remained chaste. Some of them even went so far as to allow the bodily expression of their spirit to perish. This was the « endura », which hastened death and which was considered as true deliverance. Purification rites (« katharos » in Greek means « pure ») by the laying-on of hands, the so-called « consolamentum », replaced Roman Catholic baptism. There were no sacraments, and the rites and beliefs of the Roman Catholic church were ridiculed. The licentious lifestyle of the church's clerks and prelates also came in for severe criticism.

The Cathars existed all over Europe, under a variety of names (Patarins in Italy, Pifles in Flanders). Yet only in Languedoc did the heresy become deeply rooted and it was here that it first gained success. The mediocrity of some of the local clergy helped the new ideas along. Berenger, Archbishop of Narbonne, « knew no other god than money and had a purse where his heart should have been », as Pope Innocent III put it. The general indifference of the population also enabled Catharism to develop. Carcassonne's Bishop so annoyed the town's bourgeoisie when he denounced Catharism as being very dangerous that everybody began to avoid the « bore ». So it was that in 1167 the town's heretics were able to take as their Bishop the « Perfect » Guiraud Mercier, without fear of reprisal, and were able to organise quite openly a church rivalling that of Rome. The feudal lords were, indeed, delighted to see the clergy under attack for, since the days of the Gregorian reform, the churchmen had escaped their authority and were grudging when it came to paying tithes and other ecclesiastical taxes which they had taken for themselves. Trencavel's people provided shelter for the Good Men (or bonshommes) and listened willingly to their sermons even if they were not converted to Catharism. Guilhem Peyre de Brens, seneschal of the Albi Region for the Trencavels, refused a Christian burial and asked to be laid to rest among the « Good Men ». Bertrand de Saissac, Roger II Trencavel's closest friend and his son's tutor, ill-treated the monks in Alet Abbey and was considered as an expert in the Cathar doctrine. Roger II himself, Viscount from 1167 to 1194, was excommunicated for a while because his behaviour towards the Church was so brutal and unscrupulous. His son, Raymond Roger, seems to have been brought up in the Roman Catholic faith. Yet, his tolerance or his taste for debate led him to give permission for the Cathar Bishop of Carcassonne, Bertrand de Cimorre, and eleven codisciples to face twelve representatives of the Roman Catholic church in a «symposium». Among the Catholics were Brother Ralph and Peter of Castelnau who were papal legates. The entire Court was present at the «debates» which were chaired by the King of Aragon who happened to be passing through the town (1204). The king declared the «Good Men» to be heretics but they were nevertheless considered to be worth listening to and they went on explaining their doctrine. Pierre Roger de Cabaret, one of the Vis-count's closest advisers, even welcomed them warmly to his castles in Lastours.

How many heretics were there in Carcassonne and its suburbs? It is impossible to tell. By way of comparison, when the Crusaders arrived in Béziers, the Bishop drew up a list of some 220 Cathars and sympathisers. A similar figure would seem to be plausible for Carcassonne.

The Crusade: the siege of 1209 and the surrender

The murder of the papal legate Pierre de Castelnau on 14th January 1208 unleashed Innocent III's fury against Raymond VI of Toulouse. The Pope called for a crusade. Faced with imminent danger, Raymond VI submitted and made amends. He went even further than that; he took up the Cross. Under these circumstances, who was to be punished? Who could the Crusaders fight? The song of the crusade gives the answer to these questions. «They thought they would capture Toulouse but the town had already made its peace. So they said they would take Carcassonne and the Albi Region». Raymond Roger Trencavel was 24 years old. He was a Roman Catholic but heresy was rife on his territory, so it was the young Viscount who paid the price.

In Béziers, an ill-timed move by the defending forces enabled the footsoldiers to enter the town. There was dreadful carnage. The town was nothing but a pile of smoking ruins when, on 26th July 1209, the army of crusaders set off for Carcassonne. The Viscount had gathered together as many knights as possible. In an effort to complete the fortifications and to improve those already in existence, the canon's refectory and undercroft were demolished and the choir stalls were removed from the cathedral. This provided additional building material. The siege began on 1st August. Raymond Roger was young and impetuous. He suggested an immediate sortie but Pierre Roger de Cabaret dissuaded him from wasting his troops in this way. On the third day, the crusaders took one of the suburbs, the one with the least fortifications. For a description of what happened next, listen to Pierre des Vaux de Cernay, the nephew of one of the clergy leading the crusade: « On the following day, our forces approached the ramparts of the second suburb and launched an attack. The Viscount and his troops defended themselves with such courage that our men had to retreat from the moat under a hail of stones. During the batttle, one of our knights received a broken leg. He remained in the moat for nobody dared to try and rescue him because of the stones that continually rained down. However, one brave man, the Count of Montfort, jumped into the moat accompanied only by an equerry and saved the wounded man at great personal risk. Once this was done, the crusaders

set up machines called « trebuchets » (a sort of catapult) so as to demolish the walls of the suburb. When the trebuchets had damaged the top of them, the crusaders brought to the base of the walls, with some difficulty, a four-wheeled chariot covered with cowhide beneath which specialists were to sap the ramparts. The chariot was soon destroyed by the enemy who threw down fire, wood and stones, but the sappers took shelter in the niche they had already dug thus avoiding delay in the completion of their task. At daybreak, the wall collapsed and our troops entered the breach, making a lot of noise as they went. The enemy retreated initially to the higher ground in the walled town but, seeing our knights leave the suburb and return to their tents, they came back out of the town and began to give chase to the dawdlers, killing those who were unable to leave the suburb in time, and setting fire to all the buildings before going back to the high ground ».

Thus, after only a few days of fighting, both suburbs were destroyed. But the town within the mighty wall had not yet come under attack. Each side was considering its position. The crusaders feared a long siege which would cost them dearly in manpower. They wanted to capture the town intact, for they had already lost too much booty. What was the use of finding oneself master of a pile of blackened ruins ? Within the town, the situation was critical. Women, children, peasants from the surrounding countryside, and inhabitants of the suburbs were living in very cramped and dreadfully unhygienic conditions. It was the middle of August, and the people of Carcassonne could no longer reach either the R. Aude nor the fountains in the suburbs. Would the town's wells be sufficient to provide water for a large population ? Moreover, there would be no help from outside the town. Last but not least, the terrible massacre of the people of Béziers was present in everybody's mind. Each side, then, had good reason to negotiate. What was said ? What really happened ? The texts are vague or silent. By the 15 th August, everything was over. Raymond Roger surrendered personally to the crusaders and was taken prisoner. But his sacrifice saved the population. « The middle classes and the knights who were staying there, the ladies and damsels, were able to leave the town at their will... They left empty-handed, at speed, dressed only in their shirts and breeches. Some went to Toulouse, others to Aragon or Spain ; some set off Northwards, others Southwards ».

In the hope that the Viscount's people would return, their wealth was hidden in the courtyard of the castle. Three « treasure troves » have been found in the North-west corner of the courtyard, i.e. some twenty Carcassonne deniers and oboles minted in the reign of Raymond Roger, and a short distance away a sandstone vase containing two kilos of Melgorian deniers. Finally, still in the same area, there were piles of 20-30 conglomerate coins. It would seem, then, that for some the war was not over. Carcassonne was not lost for all time. But once they had captured the walled town, the crusaders were justified in believing that they were the masters of the region.

The West end of the town : the view towards the Pyrenees. The steep slope enabled the builders to place the two walls so close together that the square Bishop's Tower (in the middle distance) passes over the tilt-yard creating a whole group of defences in one spot.

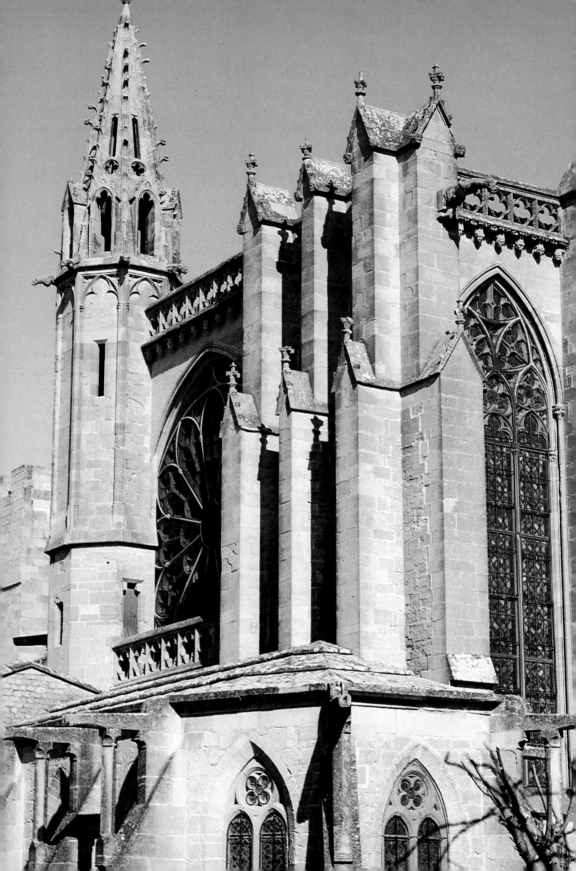

Simon de Montfort,
the new Viscount of Carcassonne

Under pressure from the papal legate, the town, all its wealth and the Trencavels' lands were given to one of the most active lords of the crusade, Simon de Montfort. He was a brave man (he fought on behalf of God and therefore had nothing to fear, as he liked to say) and a fervent Roman Catholic who was untroubled by any scruples (the heretics were God's enemies and as such had to be destroyed). In the administration of his estates in Montfort in Yvelines in the Paris Basin (later to be known as Montfort l'Amaury), and during the fourth crusade, he showed his qualities: absolute honesty, energy, and a talent for organisation. They did not go unnoticed by his friend, the prelate Gui des Vaux de Cernay. He was also close to Philippe Auguste, and was much appreciated by the king.

Raymond Roger Trencavel died in the dungeon where he was kept a prisoner on 10th November 1209. His son, Raymond, was still only a child; he had been placed in the care of the Count of Foix before the disaster. The walled town became the headquarters of the expeditionary forces who were sent out to fight the rebel lords (the so-called «faidits») and the heretic villages. In 1215, Prince Louis, Philippe Auguste's elder son, spent the month of May in the town, accompanied by a large number of high-ranking nobles. The Cathars were actively hunted down. Those inhabitants who were under no suspicion of heresy soon returned to Carcassonne. They attended the funeral of the unfortunate Trencavel and the celebrations on the occasion of the baptism of Petronille, Simon's third daughter who was born in the town, or of the marriage of his eldest son Amaury with Beatrix of Burgundy. St. Dominic officiated at both ceremonies in St. Nazaire's Cathedral.

Gradually, the suburbs were rebuilt and each made some pretence of submission at least. It was well known that any treasonable act would be immediately put down. The «French» lived in fear of fights, assassination attemps, and ambushes. A clerk who helped the heretics was attached to a horse's tail and dragged all through the streets of the town before being hung. It was common knowledge, passed on by word of mouth, that the inhabitants of Bram had had their noses cut off and their eyes poked out, and that in Minerve 140 Perfects had been burnt at the stake. People did not forget the merciless fight against the heretics because of the «Statutes of Pamiers», a legal system promulgated by the Count that was fairly favourable to the middle classes and the peasants.

For eight years, Simon de Montfort launched campaign after campaign thereby managing to keep the region in check if not wiping out all opposition. On 25th June 1218, as he was trying to capture Toulouse, Montfort died after

The South arm of the transept in St. Nazaire's: here, as on the Sainte-Chapelle in Paris, it is buttresses and not flying buttresses outside the cathedral which take the thrust of the Gothic vaulting. In the foreground is Radulphe's Chapel which was built ten years before the reconstruction of the transept. It was originally the chapter's infirmary chapel before becoming the funeral chapel of Bishop Guillaume Radulphe in 1266.

being hit with a missile from a trebuchet. His son Amaury was unable to offer any resistance to the two powerful lords who united against him, Raymond VII of Toulouse and the Count of Foix.

At the end of 1223, Amaury de Montfort was penniless. His only support came from his uncle Gui, from Marshal Gui de Levis, and from a few dozen knights. Cornered within his own town, he managed to negotiate his departure. On 15th January 1223, he left the town and set off for his ancestral estate in the Paris Basin.* This left the way open for the son of the person who had lost all in 1209. At the age of 17, the Count of Foix' protégé proudly proclaimed himself in a charter dated February 1224 « Trencavel by the grace of God, Viscount of Béziers, Carcassonne, Razès and Albi ». His joy was to be short-lived.

* The Montforts did not then fade from the scene. Amaury's younger brother, Simon, who had inherited from his grandmother the title of Count of Leicester, was, for a short time, to oppose King Henry III of England with some success. He was married to Henry's sister. Numerous English ballads speak of him as one of the first martyrs of freedom in the face of royal justice.

Annexation to the royal estates and the building of the outer wall

In Paris, Amaury de Montfort transferred his rights over Languedoc to the King, Louis VIII, in return for the title of Constable. In the Carcassès, the Cathars again raised their heads. The Good Men, among whom was one Barthélémy of Carcassonne, preached in the fortified villages of Montréal, Saissac, and Montolieu. Perfect nunneries, identical in many ways to the Catholic convents, existed in places throughout the province. On 28th January 1226,

The stained glass windows in the apse of St.Nazaire's : the central window (dating from the early 14th Century) shows the main events in the Life of Christ. It stands between two windows depicting personalities from the first half of the 16th Century. On the right-hand side is young St.Celse who is being introduced to St.Nazaire by his mother, and above them are the Bishops St.Hilary and St.Gimer. The window on the left is devoted to the Virgin Mary. She is shown being presented to her mother, St.Anne, at the time of her birth then being taken to the temple when a young girl. Flanking the apse are early 14th-century windows depicting the lives of St.Peter and St.Paul to one side, and the lives of St.Nazaire and St.Celse to the other.

Overleaf:
The Count's Castle: The stone bridge was originally divided into two parts by a small wooden swing bridge which was a sort of rudimentary drawbridge. The castle moat, like the one round the town itself, was never filled with water. It was the difference in ground level that was to prevent enemy forces from approaching siege towers and other assault equipment. Along one section of wall, the hoardings have been rebuilt ; they are wooden galleries containing trap doors through which the defenders could fling all kinds of missiles down onto the enemy as it attempted to sap the base of the walls.

Raymond VII of Toulouse and his « accomplices », including Raymond Trencavel, were excommunicated. A new crusade was launched, led by the king.

Like most of the people in Languedoc, the Carcassonnais were tired of war. Louis VIII had got no further than Avignon when a deputation of dignitaries came to give him the keys of the city. They were not alone. The inhabitants of Albi, Saint-Gilles, Beaucaire, Narbonne, Arles, Tarascon and Orange also sought the king's clemency. Raymond Trencavel had to flee. The King placed a seneschal, Eudes le Queux, in Carcassonne and Master Clairin, Simon de Montfort's former chancellor, replaced Bishop Bernard Raymond of Roquefort who was considered to be too much of a moderate where heresey was concerned. Gui de Montfort, Simon's brother, Gui de Levis, Pierre de Voisins and other barons from the North came back to their feudal lands. In the years following the creation of the seneschalsy of Carcassonne, work was undertaken to complete the town's defensive system. However, as there are no texts available on this subject, it is impossible to date the work exactly.

It is likely that the fortified « casing » round three sides of the Viscount's castle was built at this time. The depressed arches seem a little old-fashioned whereas the rectangular layout of the building, the entrance between twin towers and topped by two storeys each with its own portcullis and machicolations, the stirrup-shaped base of the slit-windows and their staggered position that increased the angles of fire and reduced weakness in the wall's structure, are all fairly typical of the progress made by royal architects since the days of Philippe Auguste. Moreover, the fortifications built facing the town are an eloquent sign of the Frenchmen's mistrust of the local population during the first few years of royal occupation.

Equally present in their minds was the fear of attack from outside, and the protection afforded by the old Gallo-Roman wall was considered to be insufficient. The wall was therefore surrounded by a primary line of defence which follows almost the same layout as the present outer wall. Along its entire length, the medium-bonded wall has horseshoe-shaped towers open at the gorge, i.e. towards the town, so that

Top:
The South rose window in St.Nazaire's Church: The pastel tones of the rose window surround Christ in Majesty. The coat-of-arms of Pierre de Rochefort, « azure with three rooks of or two and one », are easy to pick out in the central quadrilobe and in each corner at the bottom of the window. It dates the window as early 14th Century, for Pierre de Rochefort was Bishop of Carcassonne from 1300 to 1321.

Bottom:
A fresco in the round chamber: this room in the castle (probably called The Round Chamber because of its semicircular vaulted roof, or because the Lord and his vassals were seated in a circle there as in the legend of the Knights of the Round Table) is the only one to have preserved part of its mediaeval decoration. The vaulted roof was painted blue, which was common in those days. Around the top part of the walls is a painting of a battle between the Franks and the Saracens, perhaps recalling the feats of Bernard Aton Trencavel in the Holy Land during the First Crusade or when he fought the Moors in Spain. The style of the painting, though, is rather more reminiscent of early 13th century work.

they would not provide shelter for enemy forces if they were captured.

There were many advantages to this double wall. The enemy was faced with two staggered lines of fire. The sappers' job was of course made more difficult inasmuch as they had to destroy two successive walls. Finally, between the two, was an area which was automatically unfavourable for attackers ; they had no cover, little room for manœuvre and no space to fall back in. Moreover, they were exposed to the fury of the horsemen for whom the space resembled a boulevard. They galloped along it clearing the immediate approaches to the inner wall.

The tilt-yard, as this space was known, had to be levelled. The slope of the hillside often gave it a contour that hindered the passage of man and horse.

Earth was taken from the base of the Gallo-Roman wall and carried a few yards downhill, where it was used to raise the level of the ground behind the outer wall. But the work was fraught with difficulties. The foundations of the Roman towers and wall were uncovered and it became necessary to underpin the Lower Empire's fortifications to some considerable depth. Several sections of wall collapsed, one of the towers began to slope slightly, and the next tower along acquired a dangerous list and lost its upper storey. The wall was rebuilt or consolidated, and where necessary relieving arches were erected to spread the stress over a wider area. These very obvious modifications to the North-facing wall indicate the desire to deal with the most urgent requirements although the region to the South was by no means pacified.

The revolt of 1240 : the garrison withstands attack in the town

Raymond Trencavel was kicking his heels in Aragon where he had taken refuge and was dreaming of recovering his lands. In the Corbières and Montagne Noire regions, there were a large number of nobles ready to answer his call for help. In 1240, at the age of 33, he made one final attempt. Olivier de Termes, Jourdain de Saissac, and all the others who were thoroughly exasperated by royal authority and the Church's obstinacy vis-à-vis the heretics, joined him in Roussillon. In Carcassonne, Seneschal Guillaume des Ormes began to organise the town's defences. Food and cattle were requisitioned, and engines of war were built. Messengers were sent out to Bourges where the King had his court, to ask for assistance. The majority of the town's population was « French » or at least supported the King. On the other hand,

those who had returned to the suburbs and rebuilt the areas that had been destroyed in 1209 seemed to be much less reliable.

On 7th September, the Bishop of Toulouse and the Seneschal came to appeal to the people of the suburb of Saint-Vincent who had gathered in St. Mary's Church. They all swore on the holy wafer, the relics and the Holy Gospels that they would remain faithful to the King. During the following night, some of them handed the suburb over to Trencavel.

A week passed and still the rebels had not launched an attack on the town. But with the help of the population, they dug out galleries, underground passages that were to be used in the sapping of the town's walls. Guillaume des Ormes explained how they worked : « They started to dig their tunnels from their houses so that we knew nothing about them until they reached the tilt-yard ». On 17th September, the Seneschal successfully attacked the suburb of Graveillant. During the next few days, however, Trencavel and his forces took control of the banks of the R. Aude. An artillery battle opposed a mangonel set up by Trencavel to a trebuchet brought up to position by the French. And crossbows, which were a fairly recent invention at that time, ravaged the ranks of both armies.

Up until the end of the month, the tunnelling work went on in at least five different places. It did not lead to a major offensive, however, because the double rampart then came into its own. Moreover, the town's defenders had time to build a series of makeshift obstacles beyond the sections of wall which they feared might collapse.

On 30th September, Trencavel launched a general attack — it failed. On 6th October, a second offensive was repulsed. On the 11th, hearing that Louis XI's back-up army under the command of his chamberlain, Jean de Beaumont, was fast approaching, the Viscount gave the order to retreat. The inhabitants of the suburb set fire to their houses and fled with the small troop of rebels. They knew that the King's men made sure that traitors paid a high price for their treachery.

Trencavel again sought refuge in Spain. He did not receive a royal pardon until 1247. He solemnly renounced all his rights and took part in St. Louis' first crusade. His exemplary behaviour in Egypt won for him some land in the Corbières. He spent the rest of his life there with his two sons who died without any known heirs. In the same year, 1247, the King pardoned the inhabitants of the suburbs and gave his permission for their return home. They found nothing of the place they had left, not even the ruins of their houses ; the Seneschal had had the whole area razed to the ground.

On the site of the suburb of Saint-Michel was the mighty Vade Tower, which had been built in 1245. Built over a well, and comprising its own bread oven, it is a three-storied building with ogival arches topped by two additional, floored stories. Within the wall and following its outline is a strange staircase leading to a parapet walk from which the view extends over the slopes of the former suburb of Saint-Michel. The Vade Tower is very high and round, and has a large number of slit-windows. It looks like an independent section of the town's defences. A garrison could keep control of it even if the outer wall was captured, thereby constituting a threat in the enemy's back as it attacked the second wall. The neighbouring Peyre Tower seems to have been built at about the same time. At its foot, in the moat, is a door which leads to an underground passage connecting it to the town — a discreet entrance or exit. The tunnel also leads to a well which was dug beneath the tilt-yard. All over the town, the damage caused in 1240 was carefully repaired. However, the Seneschal refused permission for any building in close proximity. In case of any future attack, the enemy was not to be allowed to advance under cover.

The creation and development of the lower town

When, in 1247, the inhabitants came back to the suburbs that had been destroyed, they were granted permission to settle on the banks of the R. Aude. In 1260, a few buildings that had been constructed too close to the town's

walls were demolished on the Seneschal's orders. The inhabitants wanted to avoid the risk of any similar action in the future so they settled on the left bank of the river. In 1262, they were followed by all the Carcassonnais who were living « outwith the town » (« extra-muros »). The new village spread out across an open flat piece of land. As is often the case for new towns, the layout adopted was very simple. It was a checkerboard around a central square. In memory of the two old suburbs, the people gathered in two parishes. To the North was St. Vincent's ; to the South, St.Michael's. The new town was circled by a humble cob wall except on the side facing the river where it was built of stone for it also served as a dyke. In the latter years of the 13th Century, building got underway on what we now know as St.Michael's Cathedral. St.Vincent's Church was built in the early 14th Century. In both churches, the chancel had a stone-vaulted roof from the outset, while the single very wide aisle had a timber roof supported on stone ribbed arches.

Like the walled town, the lower town had its consuls. Its emblem was a lamb bearing the Cross of Christ. Apart from the religious symbolism behind this choice, should it also be taken as a sign of the woollen industry which was still Carcassonne's main employer? It is quite possible. There was large-scale exporting of cloth and serge to Spain and the corporation of weavers was important enough to have its own chapel in the cathedral (St.Mathias' Chapel) as early as 1380. Carcassonne's other major industries were tanning and the sale of hides. They enabled one rich townsman, Gaufré de Merlieyras, to donate three statues for the West Door of St.Michael's, for example, and to be buried at the entrance to the church as a reward for his generosity.

The development of the new town was not completed without argument and misfortune. There was a minor dispute between the town council and the butchers who were forbidden « to kill any animal presenting a risk of infection within the town's walls ». There were more serious calamities like the epidemics for which the lepers and Jews were blamed, or the flood in 1377 when the Aude burst its banks sending water rushing through part of the town, or the Black Death in 1348, or again the Black Prince's invasion in 1355.

The Avar Postern-gate (Northern section of the Gallo-Roman wall): this is the oldest gateway into the town. The great « cyclopean » blocks of stone flanking the gate may well have come from a previous wall (round a pre-Roman hillfort perhaps ?). On the right is the exit of the sewer. The rubble wall is broken up by brick chaining. The relieving arch of white limestone and brick brings the weight of the upper section of the wall to rest on the uprights, thereby lightening the load bearing down on the lintel. All this is characteristic of Lower Empire building techniques.

Overleaf:
The tilt-yard by the Narbonnaise Gate: The strange rectangular construction backing into the inner wall seems to have contained a staircase leading down to an underground passage. (The neighbouring tower was known as the Trauquet, the « small hole, or tunnel »). This underground passage, which still exists today, leads beneath the tilt-yard to a well that never dries up and to a secret door opening into the moat at the foot of the Peyre Tower (its top is on the right of the photo).

During this episode from the One Hundred Years' War, the town was captured by the Prince of Wales' troops despite the heroic resistance of one of its consuls, Davila. He led a small band of inhabitants who had refused to take shelter in the walled town. After the usual pillage, the enemy set fire to the town. Almost all the houses, which were built of wood and cob, went up in flames. The town was rebuilt on the same checkerboard layout around the churches, which had escaped fire damage. This time, a real wall flanked by small round towers encircled it. There is a section of this wall left today; it stands against the front of St.Michael's Cathedral. In front of the wall was a wide ditch.

Despite the stone bridge connecting the walled town and the lower town, each was thenceforth to lead its own, quite distinct life.

Philip the Bold (1270-1285) makes the town an impregnable fortress

In the reigns of Philip III the Bold and Philip IV the Fair, the town was given an increasingly military appearance.

New carefully-constructed buildings, easily recognisable because of their bosses, dramatically improved the defenses of the inner wall.

The whole of the South corner was rebuilt. Among the new strongholds was the Bishop's Square Tower, which straddled the tilt-yard creating a narrow passageway that was easily defensible. St.Nazaire's Tower defended the South Gate. It contained a right-angled bend which made the use of battering rams difficult, and the enemy was forced to present itself parallel to the wall. Its right flank was left unprotected by shields and was therefore open to attack from the slit-windows in the inner wall. The South-Eastern section of this inner wall was modified as the North wall had been in the early days of the reign of St.Louis, and here bosses alternate with Roman rubble. The most impressive building project was undertaken as a result of the attempt to provide maximum protection for the East wall containing the main entrance to the town. The two enormous towers of the Narbonnaise Gate were built in the shape of a spur as this design is particularly effective in warding off repeated attacks with a battering ram. The low slit-windows enabled archers to make good use of their crossbows, a type of weaponry which had become increasingly common. Chains, deadfalls, portcullises, and heavy doors with thick wooden bars behind them formed a double device for closing the gate. The independence of the defendents was ensured by a reservoir, a salting-works, fireplaces, and a bread oven. On the second floor, the so-called « Knights' Room » was lit on the town side by fine

The Aude Gate: If you leave the walled town by the Aude Gate, you will cross two vaulted passageways which were designed to prevent the enemy gaining access to the town. From there to the foot of the mound is a picturesque path known to the locals as the « paved hill ». Since Roman times no doubt, it is the pebbles washed smooth by the river which have provided the cobbles for the main streets in the town and the surrounding area.

Gothic windows. It was designed more as a reception room than as a last defence. A rather complex system of spiral staircases led to the two upper storeys and the loft. It may well have been built with a view to confusing enemy forces.

The neigbouring Tréseau Tower got its name from the Royal Treasury (or Tax Office) that was originally housed there. Between the very sombre basement and the parapet walk at roof-level flanked by two watchtowers, there are four storeys with flagged or wooden floors. As in all the buildings from this period, the archers' positions had stone benches. From the outside, the pipe from the well-equipped latrines on the second floor is quite visible against the North wall. On the town side, the flat wall rises to a strange Flemish gable designed by royal architects who may well have come from the North of France. The Roman wall beyond the Tréseau Tower was deemed to be too weak despite alterations during the reign of St.Louis. It was demolished down to ground level and now stands slightly back from a tall, mighty, homogeneous wall which afforded better protection for the section that the gentle slope of the hillside made easily accessible to enemy troops. Further North, the steep slope meant that the building projects completed under Louis IX were still sufficient to meet the needs of the day.

The scale of the construction work can doubtless be explained by the paramount importance that Philippe III's foreign policy placed on relations with Spain and the desire to show French might in this frontier region. In 1272, the King stayed in Carcassonne at the head of a large army, when he came South to put down a rebellion led by the Count of Foix. In 1276, wide-ranging military manœuvres prepared the way for an expedition which went as far as the foothills of the Pyrenees. This time, the French army was intervening in Castilian affairs, the succession to the throne.

Finally, in 1285, came the « Aragon Crusade ». Charles of Anjou, the King's uncle, had been hounded out of his Southern Italian kingdom by Peter III of Aragon (the so-called Sicilian Vespers Affair of 30th March 1282) and his ally Pope Martin IV. Charles called on Philippe III to avenge him. For this the first conquest that the Capetians had ever attempted outside France's natural frontiers, the crusading army was certainly the largest that any French monarch had ever led.

The walled town of Carcassonne, being near the Spanish border, was one of the vital bridgeheads during the expedition but the war was soon over. The destruction of the French fleet before it could land its supplies, and the Black Death which swept through the army's ranks, led to a swift retreat only two months after the crossing of the Pyrenees. The King too fell ill, and died in Roussillon on the way back home.

The castle hoardings: this photo shows quite clearly the overhang of the wooden galleries and trap-doors through which the enemy at the foot of the walls could be attacked. All along the battlements you can see the holes cut out for the beams that supported these movable galleries. In more modern fortifications, i.e. those built from the 14th Century onwards, fire-resistant stone corbels replaced the hoardings; they are the machicolations which top all late mediaeval castles.

One of the wonders of Gothic architecture in the south of France: the chancel and transept of St.Nazaire

While the major rebuilding programme was strengthening the town's inner defences, St.Nazaire's Cathedral was undergoing major alteration.

In 1267, the Bishop and Chapter announced to the King their intention of building a larger chancel and transept.

The relative poverty of the diocese and a lack of space made total rebuilding impossible, so when work got underway in 1269, attempts were made to create some sort of harmony between the new parts of the cathedral and the Romanesque nave that was being preserved. The arches in the transept were supported by round or square pillars cantoned with half-columns that were reminiscent of the alternating Romanesque pillars. A fairly shallow seven-sided apse fitted in with the proportions of the nave.

The Sainte-Chapelle in Paris, which had been completed some forty years previously, certainly provided inspiration for the architect of St.Nazaire. Twenty-two large statues sculpted in the pillars show the Apostles, the Virgin Mary, Christ, and local saints such as Gimer, Nazaire, or Celse. The apse is a veritable wall of stained glass. One window depicts the lives of St.Peter and St.Paul, while the other is dedicated to the cathedral's patron saints, Nazaire and Celse. At the very end, two large 16th-century windows flank a light which still has its mediaeval designs (it depicts episodes from the Life of Jesus). The radiating chapels also contain masterpieces of stained glass.

On the Gospel side is the Rod of Jesse, i.e. Christ's family tree, while on the Epistle side is a rare design of the Tree of Life based on a poetic meditation by St.Bonaventure (the precepts of life are written in the branches of the tree, and the resultant virtues are like fruit hanging on the boughs). There are two magnificent rose windows. In the North arm of the transept, the window surrounds the Madonna and Child, while in the South arm it surrounds Christ in Majesty.

As in the Sainte-Chapelle, the walls and arches were painted in bright colours: red and white backgrounds with purples, blues, and yellows for the clothes. Today, in the arch above the chancel, one can just make out Christ on the Day of Judgement and the symbols of the four Evangelists.

The alterations were practically completed under Bishop Pierre de Rochefort whose coat-of-arms (three rooks from a chessboard) decorate some of the keystones and the centre of the South rose window. The Bishop died in 1321 and was buried in the chapel that he had built at one end of the North side aisle. His tomb is one of the best pieces of sculpture in the cathedral.

The tomb of Guillaume de Radulphe, which is less well-made and is some fifty years older, is a reminder of the success of this serf from the Carcassès (his real name was Razouls) who climbed all the rungs of the episcopal ladder in the reign of St.Louis, finally being made a Bishop.

The castle's curtain walls and the hoarding: In the 12th Century, it was common to build a hoarding on the walls and towers in case of attack in order to provide better protection for the defenders and to give them a chance of flinging missiles down vertically off the top of the walls. According to one of the tales of the crusade against the Albigensians, it was in just such a gallery that Raymond-Roger Trencavel was standing when he saw the huge army of crusaders in the distance.

The people of Carcassonne v. the Inquisition

In the Gothic transept of St.Nazaire's Cathedral is another, humbler tomb embedded in the wall below the North rose window. It too merits our attention (cf. René Nelli, « The Cathars », pub. by Ouest-France). Beneath the tombstone lies Sans Morlane, archdeacon of Carcassonne, who was at one time accused of heresy by the Inquisition. A Cathar at heart though forced to hide his faith, a man who was « understanding » where the Perfects were concerned or who was simply opposed to the excesses of the Inquisition, Sans Morlane was one of the many town dignitaries who came up against the Dominicans. In 1283, he took part in a conspiracy that still sounds strangely modern. At that time, the Inquisition's registers were kept scrupulously up to date and therefore constituted a dangerous file. All those who were suspected of heresy, all those who had helped, been friendly with, or hidden heretics, and all those who had simply omitted to denounce sympathisers were liable to arrest. A secret threat, then, hung over the majority of the people. A small group of dignitaries, consuls and men of the robe decided to get rid of the terrible file. The registers were doubtless kept in the Justice Tower, or on the nearby premises of the Inquisition, or in the tower that bore its name. The conspirators convinced a servant, Bernard Lagarrigue, to steal the documents that inspired the townspeople with such fear and trembling. He was given a large sum of money to shore up his courage but the first snag then came to light. Lagarrigue admitted that he was illiterate. He could easily have stolen whatever he first laid his hands on. An accomplice was found, one Bernard Agasse, a professional copyist. Everything was ready. Yet the conspiracy got no further. The Inquisitor left for Toulouse, taking with him the key of the chamber where the archives were kept.

Three years later, the Dominicans maintained the same oppressive hold on Carcassonne. The consuls wrote to Philip the Fair in the following terms : « The deplorable result of this oppressive regime is mass emigration from the King's lands, depopulation, and ruin ». What risks were involved ? Occasionally, being burnt at the stake. More often, a term of imprisonment. The prison stood between the R. Aude and the town. It was known as « The Wall ». Prisoners were sentenced to "strict imprisonment", i.e. life imprisonment on a diet of bread and water, or "more lax imprisonment" in a common room with the right to exercise, to tend a vegetable garden, to have visitors, to return home for short periods in case of illness, or to be given remission if one's family was left in dire straits. Charitable measures alternated with dreadful cruelty. In 1325, Guillemette Tournier was burnt at the stake in Carcassonne. She had been sentenced to "strict imprisonment" and had confided her deep-rooted hatred of the Church to an informer who had been placed in the next cell for just this purpose. For those who were freed, punishment continued. They had to wear a cloth cross and they lost all their possessions. It was said that because of their greed and their desire to lay hands on large inheritances, the Inquisitors even began to bring the dead to justice. In 1300, they made enquiries into Castel Faure, one of the local dignitaries who had died twenty-two years previously.

The Dominicans were opposed by the Franciscans. Their Lector, Bernard Délicieux, was a bitter enemy of the order founded by St.Dominic. At one time, the authorities put in place by the King seemed to disown the Inquisitors. The people of Carcassonne were overjoyed. The Dominicans could not step outside the door « without being followed by mocking cries of "caw-caw" like bands of crows ». Bernard Délicieux assembled a rowdy mob in the cloisters of the monastery. The Inquisition was booed, people ran off to free prisoners and the houses of some erstwhile informers were pillaged. The whole lower town had reached boiling point. Consul Elie Patrice « who was considered as the little monarch of Carcassonne » led the rioters. He even opened negotiations with the King of Aragon's son. In return for chasing the Dominicans out, the prince would receive the whole area. But things turned out badly.

Philippe the Fair refused to accept that the people took things into their own hands, or that the dignitaries dared to speak of their discontent during a royal visit, or that they had even considered looking for a better sovereign. For a while the lower town lost its consul and its privileges. Elie Patrice and fifteen other dignitaries from Carcassonne were hung, and Bernard Délicieux was sentenced by the Court of Rome to life imprisonment.

The town is given a specific mission: the defence of the kingdom's south-west frontier

Throughout these years, it was the new town that was particularly difficult to control. The walled town was no longer the bustling community that it had been in Trencavel's day. It was a royal fortress and life there was rather dull, as in any other garrison town.

Under the Trencavels, as during the first few years of the French occupation, the lesser local nobility who had been entrusted with a « castellany » (the defence of one or two towers) in exchange for their lands, effected regular periods of military service first for the Viscount and later for the Seneschal. Fairly quickly, though, the feudal lords began to show less willing. As early as 1268, no more than 25 nobles out of the 42 called up by the Seneschal came with their men, and then only after a dire warning had been issued to several of them. The decline of this military service gave rise to the nomination of sergeants-at-arms, mere men of the ranks who were responsible for guarding the town and who were under the orders of a Constable. There were numerous recruits from the North of France, as shown by the Christian names that were common in the area beyond the Loire, e.g. Thierry, Richer, Edouard, Colar, Brion etc. The soldiers were lodged at their own expense in a house within the walled town. Many of them married a local girl and had families. Often, the son followed in his father's footsteps; indeed, the sons of sergeants-at-arms were given priority over the other candidates for the job. It was a much sought-after position, not for any financial reason (the wages were fairly low) but because of the prestige it bestowed, the perks, and the exemptions from tax. The sergeants already had their own association in the early years of the 14th Century. It was known as the « Brotherhood of St. Louis ». How many members did it have? How many permanent sergeants were there? On a payroll dated 1260, there are only about sixty names and each man received 8 deniers a day (as a comparison, a stonemason in Paris at that time would be earning 10 sols a week, and a sol was worth 12 deniers). Some of the nobles, however, probably still constituted an additional defensive force. One 14th-century text speaks of

200 sergeants in the walled town, each earning 12 deniers a day. These figures are quite reasonable. In the Late Middle Ages, the garrison is said to have been reduced by half to 109. Of course, in addition to the fighting troops, there were all the technicians, craftsmen, and « engineers » who worked for the Army. In peacetime, the sergeants worked on a rota system guarding each gateway into the town during the day. At night, there were always 34 of them on duty at any one time. Some kept watch from fixed positions on the curtain walls, while others were in the guard room in the Narbonnaise Gate. A few of them patrolled the tilt-yard (doing the rounds 8 times per night in the summer, and 12 in winter when the nights are longer). Their comrades on the walls were to answer their calls and report any incident. Every man was to present himself for duty in regulation dress, wearing a basnet (an iron helmet) above the camail (chain-mail hood), and armed with a crossbow and a sword. Discipline was strict and absences were punished by large fines.

The town was one of the main fortresses guarding the Franco-Spanish frontier. Roussillon was not French, and the frontier of France and the kingdom of Aragon ran along the crests of the Pyrenees more or less following the present county boundaries of Aude and Pyrénées-Orientales. The numerous castles strung out on this line of mountains (Puylaurens, Peyrepertuse, Quéribus, Termes, and Aguilar) were all modernised and enlarged during Louis IX's reign, and were proud symbols of royal authority. Fires could be lit at the top of signal towers to relay any alert to Carcassonne. The town was the impassible defensive point which was to stop any invasion in its tracks and from which a counteroffensive could be launched.

The garrison had a large arsenal at its disposal. An inventory dating from 1298 listing the material stored near the Charpentière Tower near the castle mentions various engines of war e.g. trebuchets, mangonels, ballistas, bolts, ropes, counterpoises, and siege equipment (scaffolding, ladders, stakes and picks for use by the sappers and countersappers), building equipment, objects required for tournaments (flags, flagpoles, daises, fencing, tents etc.), a large number of recipients (barrels, basins etc.), grinding equipment etc.

It was from the walled town that munitions and material were sent out for military operations. In 1234, 900 crossbows of varying types and 250 boxes of bolts of corresponding sizes were sent to Agen on the King's request. In 1345, the town supplied three dozen siege slings and accessories. The armament depot was continually being restocked with more modern weaponry. In 1412, Carcassonne saw the arrival of « a large metal bombard » which caused something of a sensation.

The tilt-yard and the St.Nazaire Gate on the South side of the town: the tilt-yard was very wide to the South. This enabled riders to sweep down on any attackers who had managed to cross the outer wall. In peace time, the yard was used as a training ground for archers with longbows or crossbows. The Southern entrance to the town passes the side of the St.Nazaire Tower. Any enemy forces were therefore obliged to advance parallel to the inner wall, exposing their flank (unprotected by shields) to fire from the troops posted behind the lower slit-windows in the wall or in St.Martin's Tower.

Overleaf:
The path up to the Aude Gate: on the West side of the town, there is a hard climb from the R. Aude up the steep slope of the hill. In the background is the Count's Castle whose defences merge into those of the town itself when seen from this angle.

Decline

In the latter years of the 15th Century, artillery replaced the older siege equipment. A century later, the cannon were so powerful that only walls protected by a thiçk bank of earth could stand up to their pounding. The walled town was ill-suited to the new style of weaponry; technically, it had had its day. Yet it retained its strategic importance for the Spanish frontier was still only a short distance away. One hundred and ten « morte-paye » (men exempted from paying taxes) ensured its protection to prevent it falling into enemy hands after a surprise attack. They were the descendents of the sergeants-at-arms who had taken up service after the annexation of the town to the royal lands. The job could be handed down. At the beginning of the 17th Century, the wages (40 sous per month - approximately four or five times less than a jobbing weaver) and the supply of a quantity of salt were insufficient for a family to live on. However, the job did not involve daily duties and it gradually became even less binding. Most of these reservists were able to work at a trade at the same time. They were wool carders, hoteliers, clerks, embroiderers, tailors, farmers, schoolmasters, drapers, weavers, stonemasons, locksmiths, bailiffs, merchants etc. A twice-yearly review, at the Feast of St.John the Baptist and the Feast of St.Louis, provided an opportunity for a stately procession to the tiny St.Sernin's Church which has since disappeared (all that remains is a Gothic window in a Gallo-Roman tower near the Narbonnaise Gate). Before attending « Mass and Vespers », the proud guardians of the town fired off their arquebuses — occasionally showing a certain lack of care as they did so. In 1619, « Barthélémie, wife of Pierre Albouy » who was watching the procession from her balcony was « wounded in the left buttock », « the said injury having happened by complete accident, without malice aforethought ».

The religious struggles of the 16th Century opposed the town, which was staunchly Catholic, to the Protestant armies. In this war of skirmishes and small-scale attacks, the walls fulfilled their role perfectly. They certainly provided inspiration for the young King Charles IX, who paid the town a visit in January 1565 with his mother, Catherine of Medicis. « So much snow fell that the young sovereign took pleasure in building a castle of snow, which was defended by the people of his house and attacked by the inhabitants of the upper and lower towns ».

In 1659, the Peace of the Pyrenees marked the final annexation of Roussillon to the Kingdom of France. The Franco-Spanish frontier no longer ran close to Carcassonne. The fortress which was already technically outdated lost much of its strategic importance. The decline of the power of Spain and the long period of peace which reigned along the border finally removed all the town's military importance.

A room in the castle, shot for catapults: their weight ranges from 90 lbs. to 213 lbs. .They come from the huge arsenal set up within the walled town in the mid 13th Century. Near the Charpenterie Tower were a number of mangonels, trebuchets and other ballista. These slings had a range of 110 yards to approximately 220 yards and they were remarkably precise (there was a difference of less than 10 ft. between two shots). The walled town was a royal fortress and as such had a large store of armaments.

Abandonment and abject poverty

In the 18th Century, the walled town was nothing more than a poor, somewhat outlying suburb of the lower town that had become prosperous as a result of the wine trade and the manufacture of cloth. The building of the South of France Canal and the hard winter of 1709 during which most of the vineyards in the North were wiped out by frost opened the way to Paris for the local wine-producers whose output was already too high for existing market requirements. Carcassonne also remained a major centre of the textile industry producing mainly "rough" fabrics, i.e. heavy, hard-wearing cloth known as « Londres» which was worn « by common mortals in the East ». And indeed, most of the cloth was exported to the Orient. Many of the town's inhabitants made their way down the hill every day to the Trivalle Royal Workshop at the foot of the mound. Many others were home-workers. The spread of « absolute » capitalism was to worsen the plight of these workers over the 19th Century. In 1838, Dr. Villermé made the following observations on life in the walled town : « Without having seen it with one's own eyes, it would be hard to imagine the abject poverty that is commonplace in this last suburb of Carcassonne where many weavers and large numbers of the lowest-paid workers from the factory live. The walled town is full of narrow winding streets, badly-built houses that are filthy inside with ground floors that are often dingy and damp, poorly-furnished logdings that are too small for the inhabitants' needs, and almost everywhere absolute misery ». The fine late mediaeval houses and the 16th century residences that are easily recognisable even today by their door surrounds, their windows and their elegant staircases at the end of dark corridors had gradually been abandoned by their owners. The lower town with its grassy square decorated with a monumental fountain, and its spacious residences like the Rolland House (mid 18th Century, now the Town Hall) attracted away all the town's dignitaries.

In about 1750, Mgr. Bezons had a huge Bishop's Palace built in the midst of very fine gardens (it is now the Prefecture, or County Hall). Was it considered a penance to live within the walled town ? Whatever the truth of the matter, Monsignor lived there only during Lent.

The castle provided offices for a few civil servants and temporarily disabled soldiers. Like the Bastille in Paris, it was also a royal prison. A short time before the outbreak of the Revolution, orders bearing the king's seal had shut away there a priest who was fond of the ladies, and a worthless young man who had been locked up at his parents' request. He used to insult his mother and steal money from his respectable family to waste in taverns.

The towers of both walls, which were left to fall derelict, gradually lost their roofs. While the moat round the lower town was filled in and made into an promenade, the moat round the upper town was filled with poor-quality buildings which leant against the outer wall for support. Where the tilt-yard was wide enough to permit it, it was turned into a street. More than one hundred houses were built, either backing onto the inner wall or extending it. The stones from the battlements were removed and re-used by anybody who liked to take the trouble to bring them down. Some of the towers became stores, workshops, or cellars in which wine could be kept at just the right temperature. In the Age of Enlightenment, as in the days of the French Revolution, local government despised this reminder of the much-scorned Middle Ages. In November 1793, a bonfire was lit with the town's rich archives. Over the next few years, there were absolutely no moves to prevent the former fortress from becoming a mere quarry. Only the strength of the walls limited this underhand form of pillage. Finally, in 1850, a decree ordered the demolition of all the fortifications.

Restoration and renewal

A scholarly inhabitant of Carcassonne, Jean-Pierre Cros-Mayrevieille, saved the towers and walls from destruction. Thanks to his action, and to the efforts of the poet Mérimée and the architect Viollet-le-Duc, the fortifictions became the responsability of what was then known as « the Fine Arts Service ».

Viollet-le-Duc had been working on the restoration of St.Nazaire's Church since 1844. He was captivated by the monument, and he observed, sketched, and oversaw the work. « I spend the whole day among numerous old women who come to confession and have abolutely no hesitation in passing their fleas on to me », he wrote to his wife. The church had been used as a fodder store during the Revolution, had been reconsecrated but deprived of its title of cathedral (which had been granted to St.Michael's in 1803), and was in a dreadful state of disrepair. The great architect required all the skill at his command to avoid its total collapse.

The town then began to come to life again. Viollet-le-Duc wrote, « I have formed a group of mainly local workmen - masons, stonecutters, blacksmiths, carpenters, sculptors, men who are used to difficult jobs, all working on the site under my direction ». Some of these Carcassonnais, like the sculptor Perrin or the architect-master mason Cals, were men of real talent. 1855 saw the start of the restoration of the fortifications. When Viollet-le-Duc died in 1879, the work was far from complete. His pupil, Boeswillwald, and later the architect Nodet were to finish off the job which still, of course, shows the master's touch.

Although Viollet-le-Duc's work has often been the subject of criticism, it has been judged much less severely over the past few years. The Romanticism of the mid 19th Century and the enthusiastic confidence of the early archaeologists left their mark on the restoration of St.Nazaire and the rest of the fortress. The taste for perfectly finished work (there is not a single merlon missing from the battlements), a strong didactic will (the hoarding has been reconstituted as it was originally), and rebuilding projects that are aesthetically pleasing but somewhat hazardous (the West wall of the castle) remove the sense of absolute authenticity from the monument. Yet Viollet-le-Duc used his knowledge to the full and he understood all the ins and outs of mediaeval military architecture.

Today, the rather fake harmony that he wanted to give the monument by bringing to the fore the 13th Century work has been rejected. The Gallo-Roman towers, for example, have been reroofed with fluted tiles which are reminiscent of the Roman tegulae and imbrices. Moreover, the slates have been replaced by flat tiles on royal buildings because the King's architects apparently used them. As archaeological research makes progress, there will no doubt be other corrections. But all this will always be a question of detail. Less than 30 % of the total town has been restored. Most of this work involved roofs, roofing joists, the battlements and the strengthening of a few arches.

At the turn of the century, the walled town had become a fabulous museum of mediaeval architecture, and as such

was a favourite stop-over point with the international jetset between their stay in Biarritz and their other annual holiday on the Riviera. Then came the spread of tourism en masse which brought new prosperity to the town. Situated as it is on the road to Spain and being a place ɪo fall back on when the wind prevents all bathing along the Languedoc-Roussillon coast, the town now receives more than 200,000 visitors every year during the four summer months.

The castle, towers, walls, and tilt-yard are state property; the remainder belongs to the town itself. Well aware of the value of their heritage, increasing numbers of inhabitants are « bringing their houses up to scratch » - and are also setting up in business.

Let those who are fond of the past not be put off by the crowds. Even at the height of the tourist season, the town is quiet before ten o'clock in the morning and after six o'clock at night and the light is at its best then too. This is the moment to walk along the rue Cros-Mayrevieille, to admire the large and small wells, to stroll through the alleyways and linger on the place Marcou before visiting the tilt-yard or going in search of the Great Canissou Tower, the Aude Gateway, the Cremade Barbican, or the Avar Postern Gate.

PHOTOGRAPHIC CREDITS

Hervé Champollion: back cover, 4-5, 10, 12-12, 15, 36-37, 56-57, 62, 64.
André Panouillé: front cover, 2, 7, 17, 19, 22, 24-25, 27, 30, 32, 34, 39, 42, 44, 45, 47, 49, 51, 55, 59

Top:
The castle seen from the West: the night-time lighting creates an unreal atmosphere which would surely be much appreciated by the Romantics who recreated interest in the Middle Ages. Here we see the West wall of the castle, a section of the outer wall, and the slope of the great barbican: a veritable tangle of walls that is further emphasised by the play of light and shade.

Bottom:
The siege stone: this bas-relief, which probably dates from the early 13th Century and whose origins are a complete mystery, is rather crudely made. Nevertheless, it tells us something of the weapons of the day (helmets, swords, shields) and illustrates a rudimentary engine of war in the bottom right-hand corner. At one end of the propelling spar, a leather pocket shaped like a sling is ready for the stone bullet that is being brought by a servant. At the other end of the spar is an elementary counterpoise. The attached ropes will be pulled taut and this will provide most of the impetus. In the top right-hand corner, a small figure being carried up to heaven in the arms of an angel represents the departed soul of somebody who was doubtless killed in battle. Some people have said that this depicts the siege of Toulouse in 1218 when Simon de Montfort was killed by a bullet projected by a catapult within the town, but there is no way of proving this attractive hypothesis.

The main events in the town's history

The geographical setting

Carcassonne controls one of the three major roads between the Atlantic and Mediterranean coasts.

Moreover, Spain is not far away.

Beyond Limoux and Quillan in the Aude Valley, the traveller reaches the passes that cross the Pyrenees. The mountains have never been an insurmountable barrier and people have gone from one side to Aragon and Catalonia on the other since Prehistoric times.

There is an even easier road along the coast, following the route taken by Heracles in the days of Ancient Greece that Domitius made into a Roman road. It leads to the Iberian peninsula via Narbonne, Perpignan and the Col de Perthus.

Carcassonne is not only a link between the Atlantic and the Mediterranean; it may also be a strategic bridgehead on the South-west frontiers of France.

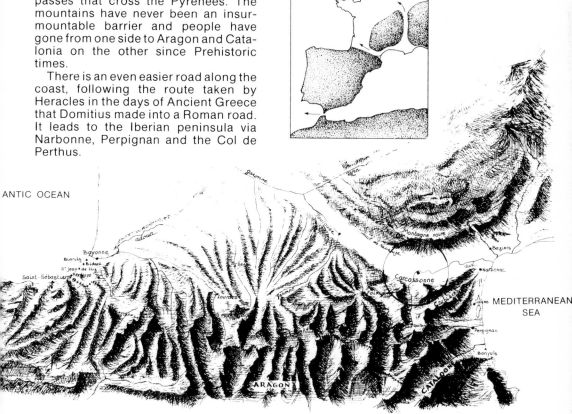

The tower of the St.Nazaire Gate: this is a massive construction in the bossed stone that was characteristic of the major alterations of the late 13th Century. At each corner are buttresses supporting, at the top of the tower, bartizans and forward towers which increased the possibilities of firing on the enemy. The small opening in the middle at the bottom is the edge of a well which could also be used from inside. The tower also had its own fireplaces and bread oven. There is a passageway on one side leading into the town.

The town as it is at present

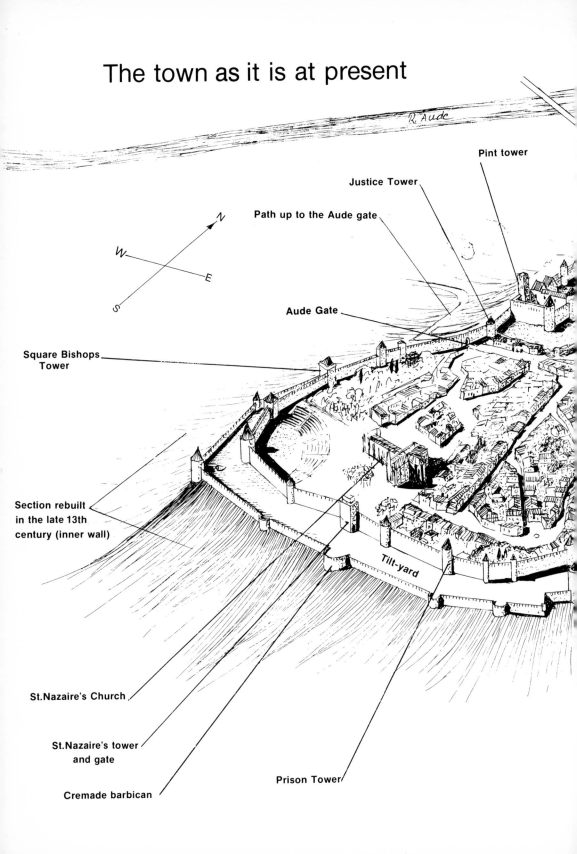

R. Aude

Pint tower

Justice Tower

Path up to the Aude gate

Aude Gate

Square Bishops Tower

Section rebuilt
in the late 13th
century (inner wall)

Tilt-yard

St.Nazaire's Church

St.Nazaire's tower
and gate

Prison Tower

Cremade barbican

N

W

E

S

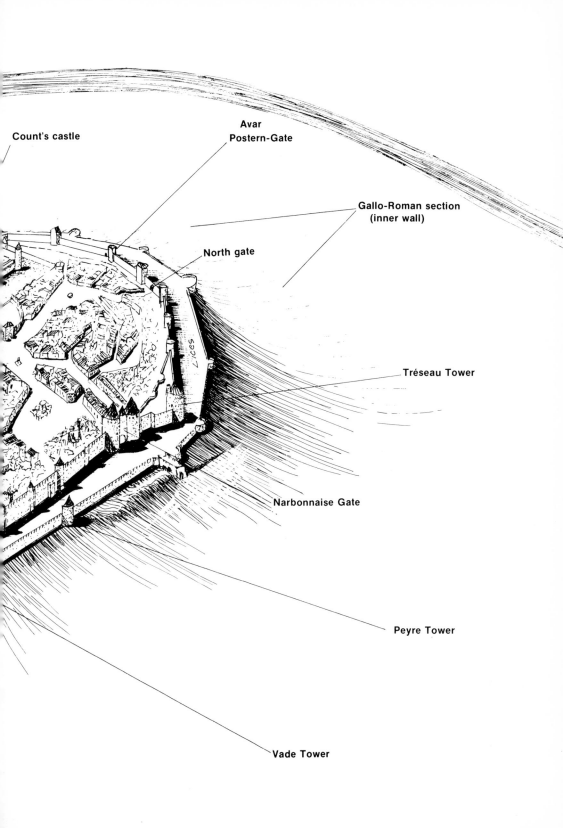

Count's castle

Avar
Postern-Gate

Gallo-Roman section
(inner wall)

North gate

Tréseau Tower

Narbonnaise Gate

Peyre Tower

Vade Tower

Evolution

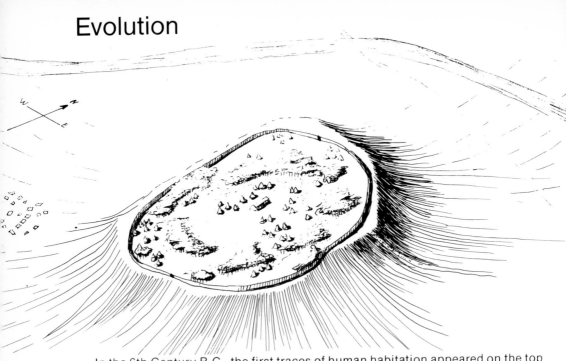

In the 6th Century B.C., the first traces of human habitation appeared on the top of the hill. This was the beginning of Carcasso, the hillfort which controlled the great road linking the Atlantic and Mediterranean coasts. It was at this time that the large settlement on the Carsac Plain (700 B.C.), where the motorway service area lies today, seems to have been abandoned.

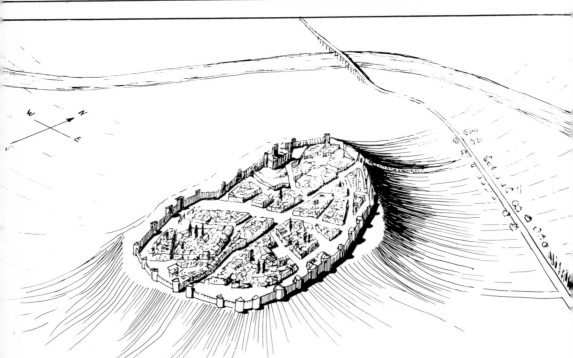

4th-5th Centuries A.D.: following on the long period of Pax Romana came a climate of insecurity which was to persist with the arrival of the Barbarians. The towns began to build thick walls for protection. First the Gallo-Romans, then the Visigoths took shelter behind fortifications, large parts of which have survived to the present day.

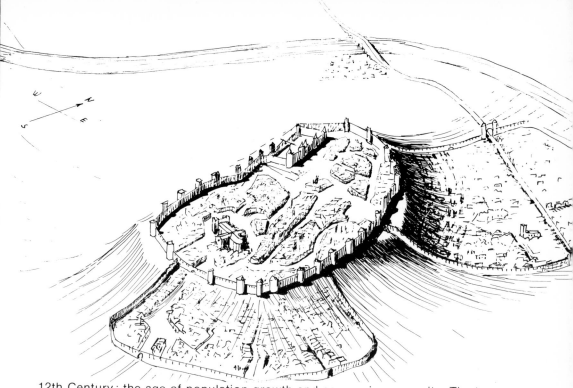

12th Century: the age of population growth and economic prosperity. The town expanded far beyond the walls to the slopes of the hill. The two suburbs of Saint-Michel and Saint-Vincent flank the old town.

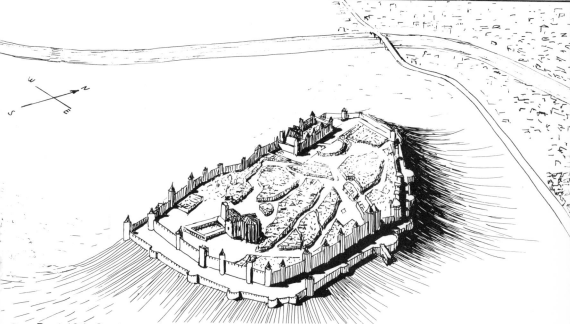

O   Post 13th Century : the town was first a fortress in the territory that the Capetian monarchs annexed after the crusade against the Albigensians and later a watchtower on the Franco-Spanish border. Kings Louis IX and Philippe III of France then made it one of the most comprehensive examples of mediaeval fortifications. The suburbs hindered active defence and were razed to the ground. A new town sprang up on the other bank of the Aude and became the centre of trade and craftsmanship.

Gallo-Roman or Visigothic fortifications?

The fortifications: built by the Gallo-Romans or the Visigoths?

Although the rubble and brick-chained walls and towers are very similar to Gallo-Roman constructions dating from the Lower Empire (3rd-4th Centuries), they have long been thought to be the work of the Visigoths (5th-6th Centuries).

Carcassonne's strategic position in the early years of the 5th Century when the only remaining Visigoth territory in Gaul was Languedoc would justify the building of a mighty defensive wall designed to ward off attacks by the Franks and the Burgundians.

Using local workmen and basing their work on Gallo-Roman building practices, the Visigoths could be said to have «plagiarised» the architecture that was typical of the land they had conquered.

Over the last few years, archaeologists have raised doubts as to the Visigoths'capabilities with regard to the building of such an elaborate system of defence round Carcassonne. Very little architecture has survived from this period. It seemed logical to date the walls from the Lower Empire inasmuch as they presented all the characteristics of the buildings of the day. A comparison with the **castellum** (or fortress) in Le Mans where the remains have been dated from the late 3rd Century and are very similar to those in Carcassonne fostered the belief that the fortifications of the Southern French town had also been built at that time. Towns in Gaul were indeed becoming increasingly safety-minded, building walls to withstand the waves of an invasion and more generally, to provide protection against the climate of insecurity that was rampant during the Empire's decline.

Yet in Carcassonne, there were a few intriguing details. Why did the walls not follow a geometric pattern as in traditional Roman architecture? Why was the facing work less well-done than in Le Mans or Senlis for example? Why was the brick chaining laid out so irregularly? Was this a sign of the rather clumsy use of techniques that were already beginning to be lost? There is no proof of this and the above observations are insufficient to modify the date of building. Nevertheless as a result of these anomalies, archaeologists tend not to make categorical statements about Carcassonne.

The reader may well wonder why the famous Carbon 14 test has not yet provided the answer. The test, however, is used to date mainly organic matter such as wood, skin, textiles, horn, bones etc. and it is not precise enough (there is a margin of error of approximately one hundred years). More modern laboratory methods, especially those concerned with the dating of pieces of pottery (and therefore of bricks) using thermoluminescence, might give some interesting results. Let us just say in the meantime that scientists still have a lot to do in the walled town (1).

Le Mans: the Roman wall

(1) Chronology buffs have come nowhere near the end of their difficulties in Carcassonne. As the castle archives were burnt during the French Revolution, it is just as difficult to date the mediaeval walls with absolute precision.

The invasions

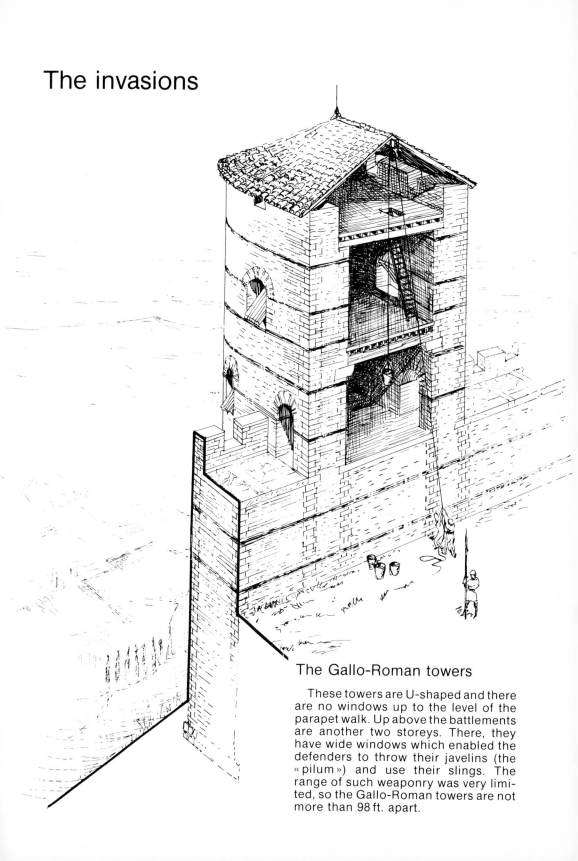

The Gallo-Roman towers

These towers are U-shaped and there are no windows up to the level of the parapet walk. Up above the battlements are another two storeys. There, they have wide windows which enabled the defenders to throw their javelins (the «pilum») and use their slings. The range of such weaponry was very limited, so the Gallo-Roman towers are not more than 98 ft. apart.

The town and its suburbs in the days of the Trencavels (12th Century)

In the 12th Century, the town was flanked by the suburbs of Saint-Michel and Saint-Vincent and its only protection was the Lower Empire wall. To North and South, the hillside was covered with buildings that huddled against the ramparts. These buildings were probably less sound, structurally-speaking, than the Gallo-Roman wall against which they leant.

The urban settlement as a whole, walled town and suburbs, knew real prosperity during this period, thanks to the weaving of wool from the Montagne Noire and the Pyrenees, the tanning trade, river traffic along the Aude from Narbonne, and the cartloads of goods that passed along the Naurouse Ridge and up to Toulouse.

Catharism met with considerable success among the inhabitants of Carcassonne. The « Good Men » or « Per-fects » preached the new doctrine without interference from the Viscounts of Trencavel who did nothing to defend the Roman Catholic religion nor to prevent the spread of heretical beliefs. Their passive attitude and their failure to fulfil their rôle as the secular arm of the Church resulted in the crusade of 1209, but it has to be said that many were perhaps attracted by the prospect of a ride through rich territory that was not far from their own doorsteps.

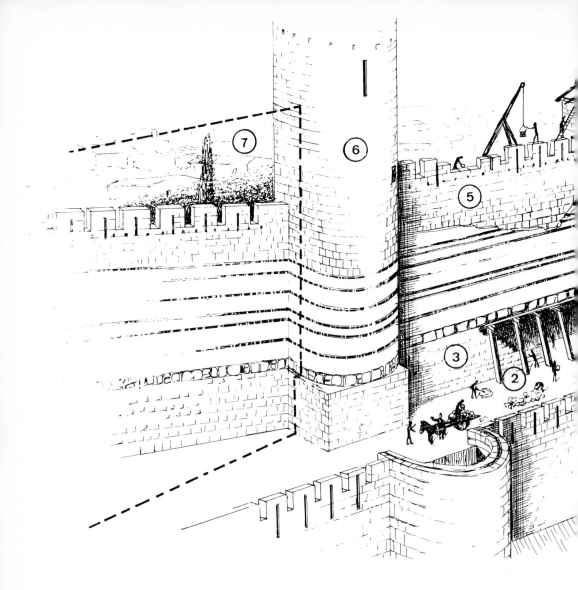

A new system of defence
(the major construction projects
of the early 12th Century)

In the reign of St.Louis or probably during the regency of his mother, Blanche of Castille, to be more precise, the town was encircled by a second wall. Here we see the work carried out on the North-eastern section near the Narbonnaise Gate and the Tréseau Tower.

The space between the two walls (the tilt-yard), which originally followed the contours of the mound, was levelled out (1). With the removal of the bank of earth at the foot of the Gallo-Roman walls, their foundations were uncovered as was the ground on which they stood. If they were left like this, it would

easy for enemy troops to dig into the soft earth beneath the masonry once they had entered the yard and undermine the inner wall. The wall had therefore to be extended downwards, i.e. it had to be underpinned (2) to a certain depth so that from the outside it was one solid mass of stone (3).

This underpinning proved to be dangerous on occasion. Some sections of the wall and some of the towers could not stand up to the clearing of their foundations and they began to lean (4). Some even collapsed altogether. The weak parts were rebuilt and strengthened, and the upper section of the wall was raised (5). Nowadays, the Gallo-Roman wall, which is easily recognisable with its rubble and brick chaining, is usually hemmed in by the 13th century rebuilding work.

Fifty years later, the architects working for Philippe the Bold (1270-1285) decided that the town was insufficiently protected, especially on the East side where the hillside had a gentle slope and there was an increased risk of attack. They it was who designed the massive defensive system of the Narbonnaise Gate and the Tréseau Tower. An impressive bossed stone wall (7 - shown as a dotted line) was thereafter to be built up to the Constable's Mill Tower (6), on the outside of the Roman wall which had previously been modified.

The battle for control of the town
(the siege of 1240)

During the 1240 siege, Trencavel's supporters tried to dislodge the royal garrison in the town with every means at their disposal. Here we see the attack in the « South-West corner » not far from St.Nazaire's Church. This section of the Gallo-Roman wall, which was probably little altered, is flanked by the newly-built outer wall.

Sheltering beneath a wood and leather shell, the sappers are digging a hole in the wall which they shore up as they go (1). When they think that the hole is deep enough and wide enough, they set fire to the wooden props and beat a retreat. Once the props have burnt, the section of wall (which is no longer shored up) collapses.

The same process can be put into effect from underground passages; it is then known as undermining (2).

An artillery battle opposed a mangonel and a trebuchet. These engines of war, which were based on Roman catapults, could fire stone shot weighing up to 110 lbs, over a distance of some 220 yds. If the spar had a sling at one end (3), it doubled the machine's range.

The impregnable fortress (late 13th Century)

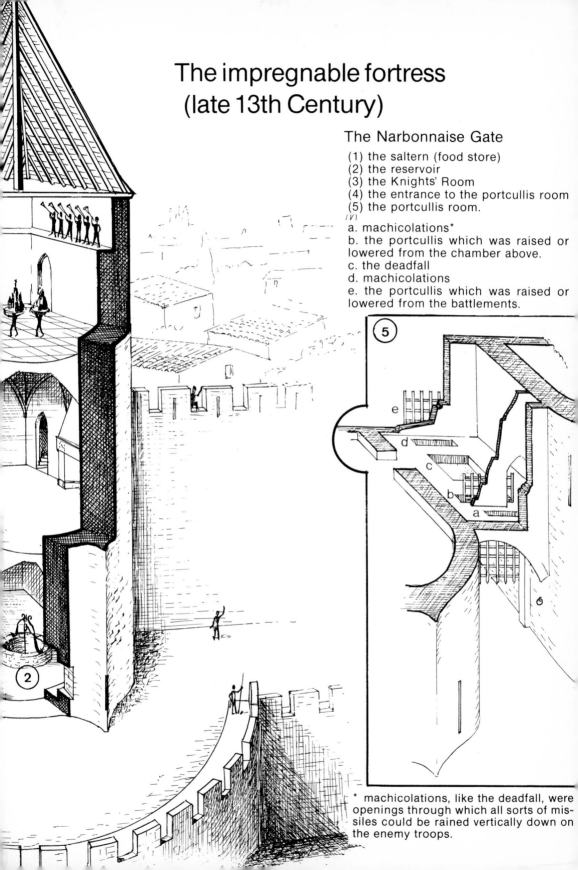

The Narbonnaise Gate

(1) the saltern (food store)
(2) the reservoir
(3) the Knights' Room
(4) the entrance to the portcullis room
(5) the portcullis room.

a. machicolations*
b. the portcullis which was raised or lowered from the chamber above.
c. the deadfall
d. machicolations
e. the portcullis which was raised or lowered from the battlements.

* machicolations, like the deadfall, were openings through which all sorts of missiles could be rained vertically down on the enemy troops.

The West wall of the castle
before and after restoration

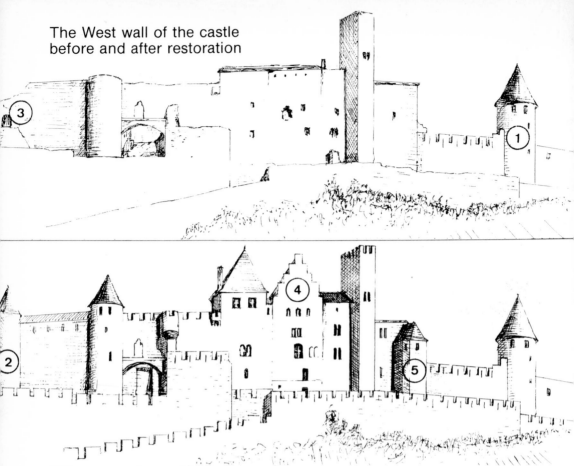

The restoration work
(second half of the 19th Century)

The first drawing is an exact reproduction of a rather fuzzy photograph taken at the end of the Second Empire. The roof of the Justice Tower (1) and the battlements along the adjoining curtain wall have just been rebuilt.

Here the castle's fortifications blend into those of the inner wall of the town.

The tower at the North-west corner (2) had to be almost entirely rebuilt. An adjutant had had an opening knocked in it, in the days before the French Revolution, in order to build a terrace onto his private apartments (3). The remains of the tower showed rubble and brick chaining; it was therefore quite logical that it should be reconstructed in the Gallo-Roman style.

The restoration of the upper sections of the main apartments is aesthetically pleasing but is probably debatable from an archaeological point of view. The Flemish gable (4) which is an exact copy of the authentic gable on the Tréseau Tower, is almost certainly a new design more than a piece of restoration. The steep slope of the various roofs is also questionable.

The outer bailey (5) is a rather unfortunate addition designed by Viollet-le-Duc's pupil, Boeswillwald.

Apart from the few « over-enthusiastic » features mentioned above, the restoration work done by Viollet-le-Duc and his successors is generally praiseworthy. It is true, though, that most of the walls and towers were already there. Only the roofs and battlements had disappeared.

Most of the work involved concerned the clearing of the walls. Since the 18th Century, many buildings had been erected against the wall and had turned the tilt-yards into real streets. Eviction and demolition was to last until 1906.

© 1984 EDITIONS OUEST-FRANCE - I.S.B.N. 2 85882 742 7 - Dépôt légal : juillet 1984 - 1020.03.12.01.90
Imprimerie Raynard, La Guerche-de-Bretagne.